Get a Grip!

"Prove all things; hold fast that which is good."—I Thessalonians 5:21.

1,000 WAYS FOR A TEEN TO HOLD ON

BY LINDSAY AND MARILYN TERRY

Post Office Box 1099 • Murfreesboro, Tennessee 37133

Printed and Bound in the United States of America

CONTENTS

PREFACE

The experiences that Marilyn and I have had with teenagers have been varied and have covered a long period of time. Thousands of teens have come into our lives as school students, choir members, Sunday school members, athletic team members, art students, special group singers, employees, participants in counseling sessions, and as our own children. Our journey with them has been educational and rewarding indeed.

The one thing that we have learned in working with teens is that our words and our wisdom are of no consequence when compared to the Word of God in their lives. Since we can only talk with a limited number of teens in person, it is with great anticipation that we prepare this volume, hoping and praying that it will touch the lives of a multitude of young people.

The Lord has allowed us to work with teens in some of the leading churches in America, and this has given us the opportunity to observe and work with teens in great numbers—wonderful, talented teenagers with more challenges, predicaments and goals than you can shake a stick at.

In our years with teens, we have led many of them to Christ. On numerous mission trips abroad, we have cooked for them, eaten with them, slept on the ground with them and traveled in planes, trains, boats, trucks, cars and buses with them. We have counseled them, played with them, prayed with them, prayed for them, taught them, cried with them and laughed with them—and at them. We have scolded them, praised them, threatened them and hugged them. We have seen them progress and grow, giving their lives in service to Christ.

In this book we have tried to list the leading areas of concern in the lives of most teens. Along with those subjects, we have compiled Scripture passages and single verses which are forceful and enlightening, and which can be used to guide their lives. The Bible says:

"For the word of God is quick, and powerful, and sharper than any twoedged sword, piercing even to the dividing asunder of soul and spirit, and of the joints and marrow, and is a discerner of the thoughts and intents of the heart."—Hebrews 4:12.

As a Christian teenager, you should tuck away certain of these gems into your heart by committing them to memory. If you have never trusted Christ as your personal Saviour, then you can find out how to know Him by reading the Scriptures found in the chapter titled "Conversion." The Bible not only lights your world, but as the Sword of the Spirit, it provides you with a weapon against Satan.

As you read the Scriptures addressing varying subjects, you will get the concept and the assurance that each passage or verse is supported and enhanced by the preceding and the following ones.

Teen, may this book be a constant help to you as you refer to it from time to time. It should not take the place of your regular Bible study, but it can be of special help in particular times of need. It can also prepare you to help others who may possess some of the same needs that you've experienced in your life.

GOD'S PLAN FOR MY SALVATION

In order to know Christ as my Saviour, I must acknowledge the truth of the following:

1. I must realize that in my present condition I am a sinner before God.

"For all have sinned, and come short of the glory of God."—Romans 3:23.

"As it is written, There is none righteous, no, not one."—Romans 3:10.

2. I cannot save myself from eternal punishment in Hell.

"For the wages of sin is death; but the gift of God is eternal life through Jesus Christ our Lord."—Romans 6:23.

"And as it is appointed unto men once to die, but after this the judgment."—Hebrews 9:27.

3. Christ has paid for my sins and taken my punishment with His death on the cross.

"But God commendeth his love toward us, in that, while we were yet sinners, Christ died for us."—Romans 5:8.

"For God so loved the world, that he gave his only begotten Son, that whosoever believeth in him should not perish, but have everlasting life."—John 3:16.

4. I must accept His crucifixion as payment for my sins, personally.

"For whosoever shall call upon the name of the Lord shall be saved."—Romans 10:13.

*"But as many as received him, to them gave he power to

become the sons of God, even to them that believe on his name."—John 1:12.

If you believe the above Scriptures, would you bow your head right where you are, right now, and ask Christ to come into your heart and save you? Turn your whole life over to Him as Lord.

You might pray something like this:

Dear Lord Jesus, I confess that I am a guilty sinner and that I need to be saved. I believe that You died on the cross to pay my sin debt. Please forgive my sins, come into my heart and save my soul. I turn my life over to You right now. Help me to live for You the rest of my life. Amen.

If you have received Christ as your personal Saviour, welcome to the family of God! Please find a good church where the Bible is taught and tell the pastor what you have done. Begin to tell others about your newfound faith in Christ.

ABORTION

To bring to an end the life that has begun
in the womb of the mother.

"For thou hast possessed my reins: thou hast covered me in my mother's womb. I will praise thee; for I am fearfully and wonderfully made: marvellous are thy works; and that my soul knoweth right well."—Psalm 139:13,14.

"As thou knowest not what is the way of the spirit, nor how the bones do grow in the womb of her that is with child: even so thou knowest not the works of God who maketh all."—Ecclesiastes 11:5.

"Listen, O isles, unto me; and hearken, ye people, from far; The LORD hath called me from the womb; from the bowels of my mother hath he made mention of my name."—Isaiah 49:1.

"Thus saith the LORD that made thee, and formed thee from the womb, which will help thee; Fear not, O Jacob, my servant; and thou, Jesurun, whom I have chosen."—Isaiah 44:2.

"And Isaac intreated the LORD for his wife, because she was barren: and the LORD was intreated of him, and Rebekah his wife conceived. And the children struggled together within her; and she said, If it be so, why am I thus? And she went to enquire of the LORD. And the LORD said unto her, Two nations are in thy womb, and two manner of people shall be separated from thy bowels; and the one people shall be stronger than the other people; and the elder shall serve the younger."—Genesis 25:21–23.

"But when it pleased God, who separated me from my mother's womb, and called me by his grace."—Galatians 1:15.

1

GET A GRIP!

"If men strive, and hurt a woman with child, so that her fruit depart from her, and yet no mischief follow: he shall be surely punished, according as the woman's husband will lay upon him; and he shall pay as the judges determine. And if any mischief follow, then thou shalt give life for life, Eye for eye, tooth for tooth, hand for hand, foot for foot, Burning for burning, wound for wound, stripe for stripe."—Exodus 21:22–25.

"Before I formed thee in the belly I knew thee; and before thou camest forth out of the womb I sanctified thee, and I ordained thee a prophet unto the nations."—Jeremiah 1:5.

"And now, saith the LORD that formed me from the womb to be his servant, to bring Jacob again to him, Though Israel be not gathered, yet shall I be glorious in the eyes of the LORD, and my God shall be my strength."—Isaiah 49:5.

"Can a woman forget her sucking child, that she should not have compassion on the son of her womb? yea, they may forget, yet will I not forget thee."—Isaiah 49:15.

"And it came to pass, that, when Elisabeth heard the salutation of Mary, the babe leaped in her womb; and Elisabeth was filled with the Holy Ghost....For, lo, as soon as the voice of thy salutation sounded in mine ears, the babe leaped in my womb for joy."—Luke 1:41, 44.

I'll never walk the shores of life
Or know the tides of time,
For I was coming, but unloved;
And that, my only crime.

—From Ballad of the Unborn
by Fay Clayborn

2

ALCOHOL

A drug that has caused more disaster in the world
than all of the other drugs combined.

*"Envyings, murders, drunkenness, revellings, and such
like: of the which I tell you before, as I have also told you in
time past, that they which do such things shall not inherit
the kingdom of God."*—Galatians 5:21.

*"Know ye not that the unrighteous shall not inherit the
kingdom of God? Be not deceived: neither fornicators, nor
idolaters, nor adulterers, nor effeminate, nor abusers of
themselves with mankind, Nor thieves, nor covetous, nor
drunkards, nor revilers, nor extortioners, shall inherit the
kingdom of God."*—I Corinthians 6:9,10.

*"Wine is a mocker, strong drink is raging: and whosoever
is deceived thereby is not wise."*—Proverbs 20:1.

*"I beseech you therefore, brethren, by the mercies of God,
that ye present your bodies a living sacrifice, holy, acceptable unto God, which is your reasonable service. And be not
conformed to this world: but be ye transformed by the
renewing of your mind, that ye may prove what is that good,
and acceptable, and perfect, will of God."*—Romans 12:1,2.

*"And be not drunk with wine, wherein is excess; but be
filled with the Spirit; Speaking to yourselves in psalms and
hymns and spiritual songs, singing and making melody in
your heart to the Lord."*—Ephesians 5:18,19.

*"And take heed to yourselves, lest at any time your hearts
be overcharged with surfeiting, and drunkenness, and cares
of this life, and so that day come upon you unawares."*—
Luke 21:34.

GET A GRIP!

"Woe unto them that rise up early in the morning, that they may follow strong drink; that continue until night, till wine inflame them!" —Isaiah 5:11.

"Who hath woe? who hath sorrow? who hath contentions? who hath babbling? who hath wounds without cause? who hath redness of eyes? They that tarry long at the wine; they that go to seek mixed wine." —Proverbs 23:29, 30.

"He that loveth pleasure shall be a poor man: he that loveth wine and oil shall not be rich." —Proverbs 21:17.

"It is good neither to eat flesh, nor to drink wine, nor any thing whereby thy brother stumbleth, or is offended, or is made weak." —Romans 14:21.

"For they that sleep sleep in the night; and they that be drunken are drunken in the night. But let us, who are of the day, be sober, putting on the breastplate of faith and love; and for an helmet, the hope of salvation." — I Thessalonians 5:7, 8.

A man who drinks now and then, usually drinks more now than he did then.

–Unknown

4

ASSURANCE

A true belief that Christ is your Saviour for all eternity.

"For the which cause I also suffer these things: nevertheless I am not ashamed: for I know whom I have believed, and am persuaded that he is able to keep that which I have committed unto him against that day."—II Timothy 1:12.

"Let us draw near with a true heart in full assurance of faith, having our hearts sprinkled from an evil conscience, and our bodies washed with pure water."—Hebrews 10:22.

"He that hath the Son hath life; and he that hath not the Son of God hath not life. These things have I written unto you that believe on the name of the Son of God; that ye may know that ye have eternal life, and that ye may believe on the name of the Son of God."—I John 5:12, 13.

"But know that the LORD hath set apart him that is godly for himself: the LORD will hear when I call unto him."—Psalm 4:3.

"The Lord is not slack concerning his promise, as some men count slackness; but is longsuffering to us-ward, not willing that any should perish, but that all should come to repentance."—II Peter 3:9.

"He that believeth on the Son hath everlasting life: and he that believeth not the Son shall not see life; but the wrath of God abideth on him."—John 3:36.

"We know that we have passed from death unto life, because we love the brethren. He that loveth not his brother abideth in death."—I John 3:14.

5

GET A GRIP!

"For I am persuaded, that neither death, nor life, nor angels, nor principalities, nor powers, nor things present, nor things to come, Nor height, nor depth, nor any other creature, shall be able to separate us from the love of God, which is in Christ Jesus our Lord."—Romans 8:38,39.

"For whatsoever is born of God overcometh the world: and this is the victory that overcometh the world, even our faith."—I John 5:4.

"The word of God abideth in you, and ye have overcome the wicked one."—I John 2:14.

"For whosoever shall call upon the name of the Lord shall be saved."—Romans 10:13.

"For I know that my redeemer liveth, and that he shall stand at the latter day upon the earth."—Job 19:25.

"When I cry unto thee, then shall mine enemies turn back: this I know; for God is for me."—Psalm 56:9.

"I am the good shepherd, and know my sheep, and am known of mine."—John 10:14.

"Beloved, now are we the sons of God, and it doth not yet appear what we shall be: but we know that, when he shall appear, we shall be like him; for we shall see him as he is."—I John 3:2.

Assurance rests upon the solid foundation of faith in the promises of God, as found in His Word.

—Lindsay Terry

ATTITUDE

My mental approach to my daily tasks, whether
they be simple or extremely difficult.

"*Therefore hath the* LORD *recompensed me according to
my righteousness, according to the cleanness of my hands in
his eyesight.*"—Psalm 18:24.

"*It is good for me that I have been afflicted; that I might
learn thy statutes.*"—Psalm 119:71.

"*Salt is good: but if the salt have lost his saltness, wherewith will ye season it? Have salt in yourselves, and have
peace one with another.*"—Mark 9:50.

"*For we preach not ourselves, but Christ Jesus the Lord; and
ourselves your servants for Jesus' sake.*"—II Corinthians 4:5.

"*Let this mind be in you, which was also in Christ Jesus:
Who, being in the form of God, thought it not robbery to be
equal with God: But made himself of no reputation, and
took upon him the form of a servant, and was made in the
likeness of men: And being found in fashion as a man, he
humbled himself, and became obedient unto death, even the
death of the cross.*"—Philippians 2:5–8.

"*Do all things without murmurings and disputings.*"—
Philippians 2:14.

"*Rejoice evermore. Pray without ceasing. In every thing
give thanks: for this is the will of God in Christ Jesus concerning you.*"—I Thessalonians 5:16–18.

"*Wherefore laying aside all malice, and all guile, and
hypocrisies, and envies, and all evil speakings.*"—I Peter 2:1.

"For the word of God is quick, and powerful, and sharper than any twoedged sword, piercing even to the dividing asunder of soul and spirit, and of the joints and marrow, and is a discerner of the thoughts and intents of the heart."—Hebrews 4:12.

"And be not conformed to this world: but be ye transformed by the renewing of your mind, that ye may prove what is that good, and acceptable, and perfect, will of God."—Romans 12:2.

"And let the peace of God rule in your hearts, to the which also ye are called in one body; and be ye thankful."—Colossians 3:15.

"Before destruction the heart of man is haughty, and before honour is humility."—Proverbs 18:12.

"Be careful for nothing; but in every thing by prayer and supplication with thanksgiving let your requests be made known unto God. And the peace of God, which passeth all understanding, shall keep your hearts and minds through Christ Jesus."—Philippians 4:6,7.

I long to accomplish a great and noble task, but it is my chief duty to accomplish humble tasks as though they were great and noble.

–Helen Keller

BAD HABITS

Learned behavior patterns that are counterproductive
to a happy Christian existence.

*"But shun profane and vain babblings: for they will
increase unto more ungodliness."* —II Timothy 2:16.

*"Thy word have I hid in mine heart, that I might not sin
against thee."* —Psalm 119:11.

*"Having your conversation honest among the Gentiles:
that, whereas they speak against you as evildoers, they may
by your good works, which they shall behold, glorify God in
the day of visitation."* —I Peter 2:12.

*"Do all things without murmurings and disputings:
That ye may be blameless and harmless, the sons of God,
without rebuke, in the midst of a crooked and perverse
nation, among whom ye shine as lights in the world."* —
Philippians 2:14, 15.

"Abstain from all appearance of evil." —I Thessalonians
5:22.

*"For this is the will of God, even your sanctification, that
ye should abstain from fornication: That every one of you
should know how to possess his vessel in sanctification and
honour."* —I Thessalonians 4:3, 4.

*"Now we command you, brethren, in the name of our
Lord Jesus Christ, that ye withdraw yourselves from every
brother that walketh disorderly, and not after the tradition
which he received of us."* —II Thessalonians 3:6.

"Let no man despise thy youth; but be thou an example of the believers, in word, in conversation, in charity, in spirit, in faith, in purity."—I Timothy 4:12.

"Submit yourselves therefore to God. Resist the devil, and he will flee from you."—James 4:7.

"Now the works of the flesh are manifest, which are these; Adultery, fornication, uncleanness, lasciviousness, Idolatry, witchcraft, hatred, variance, emulations, wrath, strife, seditions, heresies, Envyings, murders, drunkenness, revellings, and such like: of the which I tell you before, as I have also told you in time past, that they which do such things shall not inherit the kingdom of God."—Galatians 5:19–21.

"The lip of truth shall be established for ever: but a lying tongue is but for a moment. Deceit is in the heart of them that imagine evil: but to the counsellors of peace is joy. There shall no evil happen to the just: but the wicked shall be filled with mischief. Lying lips are abomination to the LORD*: but they that deal truly are his delight."*— Proverbs 12:19–22.

"Create in me a clean heart, O God; and renew a right spirit within me."—Psalm 51:10.

The undisciplined is a headache to himself and a heartache to others and is ill prepared to face the stern realities of life.

−Unknown

BEAUTY

That which causes a person to be attractive spiritually
or physically. Our goal should be to be
"beautiful" before the Lord.

"And let the beauty of the LORD our God be upon us: and establish thou the work of our hands upon us; yea, the work of our hands establish thou it."—Psalm 90:17.

"The glory of young men is their strength: and the beauty of old men is the gray head."—Proverbs 20:29.

"How beautiful upon the mountains are the feet of him that bringeth good tidings, that publisheth peace; that bringeth good tidings of good, that publisheth salvation; that saith unto Zion, Thy God reigneth!"—Isaiah 52:7.

"He hath made every thing beautiful in his time: also he hath set the world in their heart, so that no man can find out the work that God maketh from the beginning to the end."—Ecclesiastes 3:11.

"Give unto the LORD the glory due unto his name; worship the LORD in the beauty of holiness."—Psalm 29:2.

"Favour is deceitful, and beauty is vain: but a woman that feareth the LORD, she shall be praised."—Proverbs 31:30.

"As a jewel of gold in a swine's snout, so is a fair woman which is without discretion."—Proverbs 11:22.

"For the LORD taketh pleasure in his people: he will beautify the meek with salvation."—Psalm 149:4.

11

GET A GRIP!

"Whose adorning let it not be that outward adorning of plaiting the hair, and of wearing of gold, or of putting on of apparel; But let it be the hidden man of the heart, in that which is not corruptible, even the ornament of a meek and quiet spirit, which is in the sight of God of great price." — I Peter 3:3,4.

"And how shall they preach, except they be sent? as it is written, How beautiful are the feet of them that preach the gospel of peace, and bring glad tidings of good things!" — Romans 10:15.

"When thou with rebukes dost correct man for iniquity, thou makest his beauty to consume away like a moth: surely every man is vanity. Selah." — Psalm 39:11.

"And he sent, and brought him in. Now he was ruddy, and withal of a beautiful countenance, and goodly to look to. And the LORD said, Arise, anoint him: for this is he." — I Samuel 16:12.

"Thy people shall be willing in the day of thy power, in the beauties of holiness from the womb of the morning: thou hast the dew of thy youth." — Psalm 110:3.

We would worry less about what others think of us if we realized how seldom they do.

—Ethel Barrett

CHARACTER

**Character is what you really are, while reputation
is what others think you are.**

*"But grow in grace, and in the knowledge of our Lord and
Saviour Jesus Christ. To him be glory both now and for ever.
Amen."* —II Peter 3:18.

*"And beside this, giving all diligence, add to your faith
virtue; and to virtue knowledge; And to knowledge temperance; and to temperance patience; and to patience godliness;
And to godliness brotherly kindness; and to brotherly kindness charity. For if these things be in you, and abound, they
make you that ye shall neither be barren nor unfruitful in
the knowledge of our Lord Jesus Christ."* —II Peter 1:5–8.

*"Recompense to no man evil for evil. Provide things hon-
est in the sight of all men....Be not overcome of evil, but
overcome evil with good."* —Romans 12:17,21.

*"And the Lord said unto him, Now do ye Pharisees make
clean the outside of the cup and the platter; but your inward
part is full of ravening and wickedness. Ye fools, did not he
that made that which is without make that which is within
also?"* —Luke 11:39,40.

*"The heart is deceitful above all things, and desperately
wicked: who can know it? I the LORD search the heart, I try
the reins, even to give every man according to his ways, and
according to the fruit of his doings."* —Jeremiah 17:9,10.

*"Behold, thou desirest truth in the inward parts: and in
the hidden part thou shalt make me to know wisdom."* —
Psalm 51:6.

13

"*Rejoice, O young man, in thy youth; and let thy heart cheer thee in the days of thy youth, and walk in the ways of thine heart, and in the sight of thine eyes: but know thou, that for all these things God will bring thee into judgment. Therefore remove sorrow from thy heart, and put away evil from thy flesh: for childhood and youth are vanity.*"—Ecclesiastes 11:9, 10.

"*Even a child is known by his doings, whether his work be pure, and whether it be right.*"—Proverbs 20:11.

"*Blessed are they that keep judgment, and he that doeth righteousness at all times.*"—Psalm 106:3.

"*Create in me a clean heart, O God; and renew a right spirit within me.*"—Psalm 51:10.

"*LORD, who shall abide in thy tabernacle? who shall dwell in thy holy hill? He that walketh uprightly, and worketh righteousness, and speaketh the truth in his heart. He that backbiteth not with his tongue, nor doeth evil to his neighbour, nor taketh up a reproach against his neighbour. In whose eyes a vile person is contemned; but he honoureth them that fear the LORD. He that sweareth to his own hurt, and changeth not. He that putteth not out his money to usury, nor taketh reward against the innocent. He that doeth these things shall never be moved.*"—Psalm 15:1–5.

God is more concerned about our character than our comfort. His goal is not to pamper us physically, but to perfect us spiritually.

—Paul W. Powell

14

CHURCH

Those who have given their hearts and lives to Christ.
The body of Christ. Jesus loved the church
and gave Himself for her.

"Therefore as the church is subject unto Christ, so let the wives be to their own husbands in every thing. Husbands, love your wives, even as Christ also loved the church, and gave himself for it." —Ephesians 5:24, 25.

"Not forsaking the assembling of ourselves together, as the manner of some is; but exhorting one another: and so much the more, as ye see the day approaching." —Hebrews 10:25.

"And I say also unto thee, That thou art Peter, and upon this rock I will build my church; and the gates of hell shall not prevail against it." —Matthew 16:18.

"And so were the churches established in the faith, and increased in number daily." —Acts 16:5.

"And he is the head of the body, the church: who is the beginning, the firstborn from the dead; that in all things he might have the preeminence." —Colossians 1:18.

"For as the body is one, and hath many members, and all the members of that one body, being many, are one body: so also is Christ. For by one Spirit are we all baptized into one body, whether we be Jews or Gentiles, whether we be bond or free; and have been all made to drink into one Spirit. For the body is not one member, but many." —I Corinthians 12:12–14.

15

"And they continued stedfastly in the apostles' doctrine and fellowship, and in breaking of bread, and in prayers." —Acts 2:42.

"Ye also, as lively stones, are built up a spiritual house, an holy priesthood, to offer up spiritual sacrifices, acceptable to God by Jesus Christ." —I Peter 2:5.

"And it came to pass, when king Hezekiah heard it, that he rent his clothes, and covered himself with sackcloth, and went into the house of the LORD." —Isaiah 37:1.

"And many nations shall come, and say, Come, and let us go up to the mountain of the LORD, and to the house of the God of Jacob; and he will teach us of his ways, and we will walk in his paths: for the law shall go forth of Zion, and the word of the LORD from Jerusalem." —Micah 4:2.

"Now therefore ye are no more strangers and foreigners, but fellowcitizens with the saints, and of the household of God; And are built upon the foundation of the apostles and prophets, Jesus Christ himself being the chief corner stone." —Ephesians 2:19,20.

"Praising God, and having favour with all the people. And the Lord added to the church daily such as should be saved." —Acts 2:47.

"Take heed therefore unto yourselves, and to all the flock, over the which the Holy Ghost hath made you overseers, to feed the church of God, which he hath purchased with his own blood." —Acts 20:28.

Some people are like buzzards; they rarely go to church unless someone dies.

–Unknown

CLOTHES

One of the three most important interests in
the life of the average teenager.

"And he said unto his disciples, Therefore, I say unto you,
Take no thought for your life, what ye shall eat; neither for
the body, what ye shall put on. The life is more than meat,
and the body is more than raiment."—Luke 12:22,23.

"I put on righteousness, and it clothed me: my judgment
was as a robe and a diadem."—Job 29:14.

"For we brought nothing into this world, and it is certain
we can carry nothing out. And having food and raiment let
us be therewith content."—I Timothy 6:7,8.

"And ye have respect to him that weareth the gay clothing, and say unto him, Sit thou here in a good place; and say
to the poor, Stand thou there, or sit here under my footstool:
Are ye not then partial in yourselves, and are become judges
of evil thoughts?"—James 2:3,4.

"The woman shall not wear that which pertaineth unto a
man, neither shall a man put on a woman's garment: for all
that do so are abomination unto the LORD thy God."—
Deuteronomy 22:5.

"In like manner also, that women adorn themselves in
modest apparel, with shamefacedness and sobriety; not with
broided hair, or gold, or pearls, or costly array; But (which
becometh women professing godliness) with good works."—
I Timothy 2:9,10.

"Strength and honour are her clothing; and she shall
rejoice in time to come."—Proverbs 31:25.

17

"Likewise, ye younger, submit yourselves unto the elder. Yea, all of you be subject one to another, and be clothed with humility: for God resisteth the proud, and giveth grace to the humble." —I Peter 5:5.

"But what went ye out for to see? A man clothed in soft raiment? behold, they that wear soft clothing are in kings' houses." —Matthew 11:8.

"Wherefore, if God so clothe the grass of the field, which to day is, and to morrow is cast into the oven, shall he not much more clothe you, O ye of little faith? Therefore take no thought, saying, What shall we eat? or, What shall we drink? or, Wherewithal shall we be clothed? (For after all these things do the Gentiles seek:) for your heavenly Father knoweth that ye have need of all these things. But seek ye first the kingdom of God, and his righteousness; and all these things shall be added unto you." —Matthew 6:30–33.

"But as for me, when they were sick, my clothing was sackcloth: I humbled my soul with fasting; and my prayer returned into mine own bosom." —Psalm 35:13.

"While they behold your chaste conversation coupled with fear. Whose adorning let it not be that outward adorning of plaiting the hair, and of wearing of gold, or of putting on of apparel." —I Peter 3:2,3.

**People seldom notice old clothes
if you wear a big smile.**

—Lee Mildon

COMMITMENT

A determination to live with total resolve in order
to make one's life count for God.

"Commit thy way unto the LORD; trust also in him; and
he shall bring it to pass."—Psalm 37:5.

"I beseech you therefore, brethren, by the mercies of God,
that ye present your bodies a living sacrifice, holy, acceptable unto God, which is your reasonable service. And be not
conformed to this world: but be ye transformed by the
renewing of your mind, that ye may prove what is that good,
and acceptable, and perfect, will of God."—Romans 12:1, 2.

"O Timothy, keep that which is committed to thy trust,
avoiding profane and vain babblings, and oppositions of
science falsely so called."—I Timothy 6:20.

"And they straightway left their nets, and followed him.
And going on from thence, he saw other two brethren, James
the son of Zebedee, and John his brother, in a ship with
Zebedee their father, mending their nets; and he called
them. And they immediately left the ship and their father,
and followed him."—Matthew 4:20–22.

"Into thine hand I commit my spirit: thou hast redeemed
me, O LORD God of truth."—Psalm 31:5.

"I am crucified with Christ: nevertheless I live; yet not I,
but Christ liveth in me: and the life which I now live in the
flesh I live by the faith of the Son of God, who loved me, and
gave himself for me."—Galatians 2:20.

"Being then made free from sin, ye became the servants of
righteousness."—Romans 6:18.

19

"And I sought for a man among them, that should make up the hedge, and stand in the gap before me for the land, that I should not destroy it: but I found none."—Ezekiel 22:30.

"For whosoever will save his life shall lose it; but whosoever shall lose his life for my sake and the gospel's, the same shall save it."—Mark 8:35.

"No man can serve two masters: for either he will hate the one, and love the other; or else he will hold to the one, and despise the other. Ye cannot serve God and mammon."—Matthew 6:24.

"And why stand we in jeopardy every hour? I protest by your rejoicing which I have in Christ Jesus our Lord, I die daily."—I Corinthians 15:30,31.

"Now thanks be unto God, which always causeth us to triumph in Christ, and maketh manifest the savour of his knowledge by us in every place."—II Corinthians 2:14.

"He that findeth his life shall lose it: and he that loseth his life for my sake shall find it."—Matthew 10:39.

When you have found out what the will of God is, seek for His help, and seek it earnestly, perseveringly, patiently, believingly and expectantly, and you will surely, in His own time and way, obtain it.

—George Müller

COMPLAINING

Expressing feelings of dissatisfaction or resentment,
as opposed to accepting God's sovereign
control over our circumstances.

"I said, I will take heed to my ways, that I sin not with my tongue: I will keep my mouth with a bridle, while the wicked is before me."—Psalm 39:1.

"Do all things without murmurings and disputings: That ye may be blameless and harmless, the sons of God, without rebuke, in the midst of a crooked and perverse nation, among whom ye shine as lights in the world."—Philippians 2:14, 15.

"Jesus therefore answered and said unto them, Murmur not among yourselves."—John 6:43.

"Nay but, O man, who art thou that repliest against God? Shall the thing formed say to him that formed it, Why hast thou made me thus?"—Romans 9:20.

"Where is the wise? where is the scribe? where is the disputer of this world? hath not God made foolish the wisdom of this world?"—I Corinthians 1:20.

"But avoid foolish questions, and genealogies, and contentions, and strivings about the law; for they are unprofitable and vain."—Titus 3:9.

"Therefore I will not refrain my mouth; I will speak in the anguish of my spirit; I will complain in the bitterness of my soul."—Job 7:11.

21

GET A GRIP!

"*But Martha was cumbered about much serving, and came to him, and said, Lord, dost thou not care that my sister hath left me to serve alone? bid her therefore that she help me. And Jesus answered and said unto her, Martha, Martha, thou art careful and troubled about many things: But one thing is needful: and Mary hath chosen that good part, which shall not be taken away from her.*"—Luke 10:40–42.

"*And when the people complained, it displeased the LORD: and the LORD heard it; and his anger was kindled; and the fire of the LORD burnt among them, and consumed them that were in the uttermost parts of the camp.*"—Numbers 11:1.

"*Even to day is my complaint bitter: my stroke is heavier than my groaning.*"—Job 23:2.

"*I poured out my complaint before him; I shewed before him my trouble.*"—Psalm 142:2.

"*Speak not evil one of another, brethren. He that speaketh evil of his brother, and judgeth his brother, speaketh evil of the law, and judgeth the law: but if thou judge the law, thou art not a doer of the law, but a judge.*"—James 4:11.

"*Let no corrupt communication proceed out of your mouth, but that which is good to the use of edifying, that it may minister grace unto the hearers.*"—Ephesians 4:29.

The usual fortune of complaint is to excite contempt more than pity.

—Samuel Johnson

COMPROMISE

A willingness to accept less than that which is right or proper.
A willingness to accept the decisions of others, even though
it may not be exactly what you would decide.

"But Daniel purposed in his heart that he would not defile himself with the portion of the king's meat, nor with the wine which he drank: therefore he requested of the prince of the eunuchs that he might not defile himself." — Daniel 1:8.

"But put ye on the Lord Jesus Christ, and make not provision for the flesh, to fulfil the lusts thereof." — Romans 13:14.

"I will meditate in thy precepts, and have respect unto thy ways. I will delight myself in thy statutes: I will not forget thy word." — Psalm 119:15, 16.

"Thou wilt keep him in perfect peace, whose mind is stayed on thee: because he trusteth in thee." — Isaiah 26:3.

"Abide in me, and I in you. As the branch cannot bear fruit of itself, except it abide in the vine; no more can ye, except ye abide in me. I am the vine, ye are the branches: He that abideth in me, and I in him, the same bringeth forth much fruit: for without me ye can do nothing." — John 15:4, 5.

"And hereby we do know that we know him, if we keep his commandments. He that saith, I know him, and keepeth not his commandments, is a liar, and the truth is not in him. But whoso keepeth his word, in him verily is the love of God perfected: hereby know we that we are in him." — I John 2:3–5.

"But be ye doers of the word, and not hearers only, deceiving your own selves."—James 1:22.

"Let not sin therefore reign in your mortal body, that ye should obey it in the lusts thereof."—Romans 6:12.

"Whosoever transgresseth, and abideth not in the doctrine of Christ, hath not God. He that abideth in the doctrine of Christ, he hath both the Father and the Son."—II John 9.

"Therefore we ought to give the more earnest heed to the things which we have heard, lest at any time we should let them slip."—Hebrews 2:1.

"But if thy brother be grieved with thy meat, now walkest thou not charitably. Destroy not him with thy meat, for whom Christ died."—Romans 14:15.

"Fulfil ye my joy, that ye be likeminded, having the same love, being of one accord, of one mind."—Philippians 2:2.

"We then that are strong ought to bear the infirmities of the weak, and not to please ourselves."—Romans 15:1.

Sometimes we mistake compromise for charity and put up with what we should put out.

—Vance Havner

CONFORMITY

At times commendable in a Christian;
at other times, deplorable.

"As obedient children, not fashioning yourselves according to the former lusts in your ignorance: But as he which hath called you is holy, so be ye holy in all manner of conversation."—I Peter 1:14,15.

"And ye shall know that I am the LORD: for ye have not walked in my statutes, neither executed my judgments, but have done after the manners of the heathen that are round about you."—Ezekiel 11:12.

"Whosoever therefore shall be ashamed of me and of my words in this adulterous and sinful generation; of him also shall the Son of man be ashamed, when he cometh in the glory of his Father with the holy angels."—Mark 8:38.

"Be ye not unequally yoked together with unbelievers: for what fellowship hath righteousness with unrighteousness? and what communion hath light with darkness? And what concord hath Christ with Belial? or what part hath he that believeth with an infidel? And what agreement hath the temple of God with idols? for ye are the temple of the living God; as God hath said, I will dwell in them, and walk in them; and I will be their God, and they shall be my people. Wherefore come out from among them, and be ye separate, saith the Lord, and touch not the unclean thing; and I will receive you."—II Corinthians 6:14–17.

"Beware lest any man spoil you through philosophy and vain deceit, after the tradition of men, after the rudiments of the world, and not after Christ."—Colossians 2:8.

GET A GRIP!

"I beseech you therefore, brethren, by the mercies of God, that ye present your bodies a living sacrifice, holy, acceptable unto God, which is your reasonable service. And be not conformed to this world: but be ye transformed by the renewing of your mind, that ye may prove what is that good, and acceptable, and perfect, will of God."—Romans 12:1,2.

"That ye put off concerning the former conversation the old man, which is corrupt according to the deceitful lusts; And be renewed in the spirit of your mind; And that ye put on the new man, which after God is created in righteousness and true holiness."—Ephesians 4:22–24.

"Let this mind be in you, which was also in Christ Jesus."—Philippians 2:5.

"For who hath known the mind of the Lord, that he may instruct him? But we have the mind of Christ."—I Corinthians 2:16.

"He that hath no rule over his own spirit is like a city that is broken down, and without walls."—Proverbs 25:28.

"That ye may remember, and do all my commandments, and be holy unto your God."—Numbers 15:40.

"And they that are Christ's have crucified the flesh with the affections and lusts. If we live in the Spirit, let us also walk in the Spirit."—Galatians 5:24,25.

"There is a way which seemeth right unto a man, but the end thereof are the ways of death."—Proverbs 14:12.

**We forfeit three-fourths of ourselves
to be like other people.**
—Schopenhauer

CONSCIENCE

A clear one is one of life's most prized possessions.

"That which we have seen and heard declare we unto you, that ye also may have fellowship with us: and truly our fellowship is with the Father, and with his Son Jesus Christ. And these things write we unto you, that your joy may be full. This then is the message which we have heard of him, and declare unto you, that God is light, and in him is no darkness at all. If we say that we have fellowship with him, and walk in darkness, we lie, and do not the truth: But if we walk in the light, as he is in the light, we have fellowship one with another, and the blood of Jesus Christ his Son cleanseth us from all sin. If we say that we have no sin, we deceive ourselves, and the truth is not in us. If we confess our sins, he is faithful and just to forgive us our sins, and to cleanse us from all unrighteousness. If we say that we have not sinned, we make him a liar, and his word is not in us."—
I John 1:3–10.

*"Thou wilt keep him in perfect peace, whose mind is stayed on thee: because he trusteth in thee."—*Isaiah 26:3.

*"But now in Christ Jesus ye who sometimes were far off are made nigh by the blood of Christ. For he is our peace, who hath made both one, and hath broken down the middle wall of partition between us."—*Ephesians 2:13, 14.

*"He that saith he is in the light, and hateth his brother, is in darkness even until now. He that loveth his brother abideth in the light, and there is none occasion of stumbling in him. But he that hateth his brother is in darkness, and walketh in darkness, and knoweth not whither he goeth, because that darkness hath blinded his eyes."—*I John 2:9–11.

27

"But without faith it is impossible to please him: for he that cometh to God must believe that he is, and that he is a rewarder of them that diligently seek him."—Hebrews 11:6.

"Be careful for nothing; but in every thing by prayer and supplication with thanksgiving let your requests be made known unto God. And the peace of God, which passeth all understanding, shall keep your hearts and minds through Christ Jesus. Finally, brethren, whatsoever things are true, whatsoever things are honest, whatsoever things are just, whatsoever things are pure, whatsoever things are lovely, whatsoever things are of good report; if there be any virtue, and if there be any praise, think on these things. Those things, which ye have both learned, and received, and heard, and seen in me, do: and the God of peace shall be with you."—Philippians 4:6–9.

"That ye might walk worthy of the Lord unto all pleasing, being fruitful in every good work, and increasing in the knowledge of God."—Colossians 1:10.

"I acknowledged my sin unto thee, and mine iniquity have I not hid. I said, I will confess my transgressions unto the LORD; *and thou forgavest the iniquity of my sin. Selah."*—Psalm 32:5.

"He that covereth his sins shall not prosper: but whoso confesseth and forsaketh them shall have mercy."—Proverbs 28:13.

"Confess your faults one to another, and pray one for another, that ye may be healed. The effectual fervent prayer of a righteous man availeth much."—James 5:16.

When a man says he has a clear conscience, it often means he has a bad memory.

—Bits & Pieces

CONVERSION

Each of us must come to the place in our lives when we realize
we have no chance of going to heaven apart from a personal
acceptance of Christ into our hearts to be our Saviour.

*"But glory, honour, and peace, to every man that worketh
good, to the Jew first, and also to the Gentile: For there is no
respect of persons with God. For as many as have sinned
without law shall also perish without law: and as many as
have sinned in the law shall be judged by the law."* —
Romans 2:10–12.

*"For there is not a just man upon earth, that doeth good,
and sinneth not."* — Ecclesiastes 7:20.

*"For all have sinned, and come short of the glory of
God."* — Romans 3:23.

"For the wages of sin is death; but the gift of God is eternal life through Jesus Christ our Lord." — Romans 6:23.

*"But God commendeth his love toward us, in that, while
we were yet sinners, Christ died for us. Much more then,
being now justified by his blood, we shall be saved from
wrath through him."* — Romans 5:8, 9.

*"That if thou shalt confess with thy mouth the Lord
Jesus, and shalt believe in thine heart that God hath raised
him from the dead, thou shalt be saved. For with the heart
man believeth unto righteousness; and with the mouth confession is made unto salvation."* — Romans 10:9, 10.

*"For whosoever shall call upon the name of the Lord shall
be saved."* — Romans 10:13.

29

"For God so loved the world, that he gave his only begotten Son, that whosoever believeth in him should not perish, but have everlasting life."—John 3:16.

"That which is born of the flesh is flesh; and that which is born of the Spirit is spirit."—John 3:6.

"But as many as received him, to them gave he power to become the sons of God, even to them that believe on his name: Which were born, not of blood, nor of the will of the flesh, nor of the will of man, but of God."—John 1:12,13.

"For by grace are ye saved through faith; and that not of yourselves: it is the gift of God: Not of works, lest any man should boast."—Ephesians 2:8,9.

"I tell you, Nay: but, except ye repent, ye shall all likewise perish."—Luke 13:3.

"How shall we escape, if we neglect so great salvation; which at the first began to be spoken by the Lord, and was confirmed unto us by them that heard him."—Hebrews 2:3.

"All we like sheep have gone astray; we have turned every one to his own way; and the LORD hath laid on him the iniquity of us all."—Isaiah 53:6.

Salvation is moving from living death, to deathless life.

−Jack Odell

COURAGE

The ability to fly in the face of difficulty, notwithstanding the fear that may have been activated by the difficulty.

"*I can do all things through Christ which strengtheneth me.*"—Philippians 4:13.

"*Let us therefore come boldly unto the throne of grace, that we may obtain mercy, and find grace to help in time of need.*"—Hebrews 4:16.

"*Be strong and of a good courage, fear not, nor be afraid of them: for the LORD thy God, he it is that doth go with thee; he will not fail thee, nor forsake thee.*"—Deuteronomy 31:6.

"*Only be thou strong and very courageous, that thou mayest observe to do according to all the law, which Moses my servant commanded thee: turn not from it to the right hand or to the left, that thou mayest prosper whithersoever thou goest. This book of the law shall not depart out of thy mouth; but thou shalt meditate therein day and night, that thou mayest observe to do according to all that is written therein: for then thou shalt make thy way prosperous, and then thou shalt have good success. Have not I commanded thee? Be strong and of a good courage; be not afraid, neither be thou dismayed: for the LORD thy God is with thee whithersoever thou goest.*"—Joshua 1:7–9.

"*Finally, my brethren, be strong in the Lord, and in the power of his might. Put on the whole armour of God, that ye may be able to stand against the wiles of the devil. For we wrestle not against flesh and blood, but against principalities, against powers, against the rulers of the darkness of this world, against spiritual wickedness in high places.*"—Ephesians 6:10–12.

31

GET A GRIP!

"If thou faint in the day of adversity, thy strength is small."—Proverbs 24:10.

"Fear thou not; for I am with thee: be not dismayed; for I am thy God: I will strengthen thee; yea, I will help thee; yea, I will uphold thee with the right hand of my righteousness."—Isaiah 41:10.

"Only let your conversation be as it becometh the gospel of Christ: that whether I come and see you, or else be absent, I may hear of your affairs, that ye stand fast in one spirit, with one mind striving together for the faith of the gospel; And in nothing terrified by your adversaries: which is to them an evident token of perdition, but to you of salvation, and that of God. For unto you it is given in the behalf of Christ, not only to believe on him, but also to suffer for his sake."—Philippians 1:27–29.

"And from thence, when the brethren heard of us, they came to meet us as far as Appii forum, and The three taverns: whom when Paul saw, he thanked God, and took courage."—Acts 28:15.

"Go, gather together all the Jews that are present in Shushan, and fast ye for me, and neither eat nor drink three days, night or day: I also and my maidens will fast likewise; and so will I go in unto the king, which is not according to the law: and if I perish, I perish."—Esther 4:16.

You cannot run away from a weakness; you must sometimes fight it out or perish. and if that be so, why not now, and where you stand?

—Robert Louis Stevenson

DATING

Keeping company socially with a member of the opposite sex.

"Wherewithal shall a young man cleanse his way? by taking heed thereto according to thy word. With my whole heart have I sought thee: O let me not wander from thy commandments. Thy word have I hid in mine heart, that I might not sin against thee." — Psalm 119:9–11.

"Even a child is known by his doings, whether his work be pure, and whether it be right." — Proverbs 20:11.

"Be not deceived: evil communications corrupt good manners." — I Corinthians 15:33.

"Be ye not unequally yoked together with unbelievers: for what fellowship hath righteousness with unrighteousness? and what communion hath light with darkness?" — II Corinthians 6:14.

"The integrity of the upright shall guide them: but the perverseness of transgressors shall destroy them." — Proverbs 11:3.

"And walk in love, as Christ also hath loved us, and hath given himself for us an offering and a sacrifice to God for a sweetsmelling savour. But fornication, and all uncleanness, or covetousness, let it not be once named among you, as becometh saints." — Ephesians 5:2, 3.

"Nevertheless he that standeth stedfast in his heart, having no necessity, but hath power over his own will, and hath so decreed in his heart that he will keep his virgin, doeth well." — I Corinthians 7:37.

"Let no man despise thy youth; but be thou an example of the believers, in word, in conversation, in charity, in spirit, in faith, in purity."—I Timothy 4:12.

"Rejoice, O young man, in thy youth; and let thy heart cheer thee in the days of thy youth, and walk in the ways of thine heart, and in the sight of thine eyes: but know thou, that for all these things God will bring thee into judgment."—Ecclesiastes 11:9.

"And whatsoever ye do in word or deed, do all in the name of the Lord Jesus, giving thanks to God and the Father by him."—Colossians 3:17.

"Delight thyself also in the LORD; and he shall give thee the desires of thine heart."—Psalm 37:4.

"Trust in the LORD with all thine heart; and lean not unto thine own understanding. In all thy ways acknowledge him, and he shall direct thy paths."—Proverbs 3:5,6.

"Remember now thy Creator in the days of thy youth, while the evil days come not, nor the years draw nigh, when thou shalt say, I have no pleasure in them."—Ecclesiastes 12:1.

You will become like those with whom you associate.

—Lee Roberson

DEATH

An eventuality that awaits people of all ages.

"*Precious in the sight of the* LORD *is the death of his saints.*"—Psalm 116:15.

"*For since by man came death, by man came also the resurrection of the dead. For as in Adam all die, even so in Christ shall all be made alive.*"—I Corinthians 15:21,22.

"*As righteousness tendeth to life: so he that pursueth evil pursueth it to his own death.*"—Proverbs 11:19.

"*Yea, though I walk through the valley of the shadow of death, I will fear no evil: for thou art with me; thy rod and thy staff they comfort me.*"—Psalm 23:4.

"*Wherefore, as by one man sin entered into the world, and death by sin; and so death passed upon all men, for that all have sinned.*"—Romans 5:12.

"*In the way of righteousness is life; and in the pathway thereof there is no death.*"—Proverbs 12:28.

"*And as it is appointed unto men once to die, but after this the judgment: So Christ was once offered to bear the sins of many; and unto them that look for him shall he appear the second time without sin unto salvation.*"—Hebrews 9:27,28.

"*For whoso findeth me findeth life, and shall obtain favour of the* LORD. *But he that sinneth against me wrongeth his own soul: all they that hate me love death.*"—Proverbs 8:35,36.

"For if we believe that Jesus died and rose again, even so them also which sleep in Jesus will God bring with him." — I Thessalonians 4:14.

"Beloved, now are we the sons of God, and it doth not yet appear what we shall be: but we know that, when he shall appear, we shall be like him; for we shall see him as he is." — I John 3:2.

"The last enemy that shall be destroyed is death." — I Corinthians 15:26.

"And God shall wipe away all tears from their eyes; and there shall be no more death, neither sorrow, nor crying, neither shall there be any more pain: for the former things are passed away." —Revelation 21:4.

"O death, where is thy sting? O grave, where is thy victory? The sting of death is sin; and the strength of sin is the law. But thanks be to God, which giveth us the victory through our Lord Jesus Christ." —I Corinthians 15:55–57.

Ninety-five percent of the people who died today had expected to live a lot longer.

—Albert M. Wells, Jr.

DECISIONS

The right ones are quite difficult at times, but
they are the only ones with rewards.

"And if it seem evil unto you to serve the LORD, choose you this day whom ye will serve; whether the gods which your fathers served that were on the other side of the flood, or the gods of the Amorites, in whose land ye dwell: but as for me and my house, we will serve the LORD."—Joshua 24:15.

"And thine ears shall hear a word behind thee, saying, This is the way, walk ye in it, when ye turn to the right hand, and when ye turn to the left."—Isaiah 30:21.

"Blessed is the man that walketh not in the counsel of the ungodly, nor standeth in the way of sinners, nor sitteth in the seat of the scornful."—Psalm 1:1.

"For this God is our God for ever and ever: he will be our guide even unto death."—Psalm 48:14.

"Trust in the LORD with all thine heart; and lean not unto thine own understanding. In all thy ways acknowledge him, and he shall direct thy paths."—Proverbs 3:5,6.

"Nevertheless I am continually with thee: thou hast holden me by my right hand. Thou shalt guide me with thy counsel, and afterward receive me to glory."—Psalm 73:23,24.

"A man's heart deviseth his way: but the LORD directeth his steps."—Proverbs 16:9.

"I will instruct thee and teach thee in the way which thou shalt go: I will guide thee with mine eye."—Psalm 32:8.

Get a Grip!

"I the LORD have called thee in righteousness, and will hold thine hand, and will keep thee, and give thee for a covenant of the people, for a light of the Gentiles."— Isaiah 42:6.

"Be strong and of a good courage, fear not, nor be afraid of them: for the LORD thy God, he it is that doth go with thee; he will not fail thee, nor forsake thee."—Deuteronomy 31:6.

"Thy word is a lamp unto my feet, and a light unto my path. I have sworn, and I will perform it, that I will keep thy righteous judgments."—Psalm 119:105,106.

"And this I pray, that your love may abound yet more and more in knowledge and in all judgment; That ye may approve things that are excellent; that ye may be sincere and without offence till the day of Christ."—Philippians 1:9,10.

"I have taught thee in the way of wisdom; I have led thee in right paths. When thou goest, thy steps shall not be straitened; and when thou runnest, thou shalt not stumble."— Proverbs 4:11,12.

Decision is a sharp knife that cuts clean and straight; indecision is a dull one that hacks and tears and leaves ragged edges behind it.

–Gordon Graham

DEFEAT

Excuses contribute greatly to it. A defeat is a loss that may be turned into a positive steppingstone in your life's progression.

"And he said unto me, My grace is sufficient for thee: for my strength is made perfect in weakness. Most gladly therefore will I rather glory in my infirmities, that the power of Christ may rest upon me."—II Corinthians 12:9.

"For which cause we faint not; but though our outward man perish, yet the inward man is renewed day by day."—II Corinthians 4:16.

"Pride goeth before destruction, and an haughty spirit before a fall."—Proverbs 16:18.

"He brought me up also out of an horrible pit, out of the miry clay, and set my feet upon a rock, and established my goings. And he hath put a new song in my mouth, even praise unto our God: many shall see it, and fear, and shall trust in the LORD."—Psalm 40:2,3.

"Let your conversation be without covetousness; and be content with such things as ye have: for he hath said, I will never leave thee, nor forsake thee. So that we may boldly say, The Lord is my helper, and I will not fear what man shall do unto me."—Hebrews 13:5,6.

"Come unto me, all ye that labour and are heavy laden, and I will give you rest. Take my yoke upon you, and learn of me; for I am meek and lowly in heart: and ye shall find rest unto your souls. For my yoke is easy, and my burden is light."—Matthew 11:28–30.

"For if ye turn again unto the LORD, your brethren and your children shall find compassion before them that lead them captive, so that they shall come again into this land: for the LORD your God is gracious and merciful, and will not turn away his face from you, if ye return unto him."—II Chronicles 30:9

"And let us not be weary in well doing: for in due season we shall reap, if we faint not."—Galatians 6:9.

"He healeth the broken in heart, and bindeth up their wounds."—Psalm 147:3.

"He giveth power to the faint; and to them that have no might he increaseth strength. Even the youths shall faint and be weary, and the young men shall utterly fall: But they that wait upon the LORD shall renew their strength; they shall mount up with wings as eagles; they shall run, and not be weary; and they shall walk, and not faint."—Isaiah 40:29–31.

"For a just man falleth seven times, and riseth up again: but the wicked shall fall into mischief."—Proverbs 24:16.

"The steps of a good man are ordered by the LORD: and he delighteth in his way. Though he fall, he shall not be utterly cast down: for the LORD upholdeth him with his hand."—Psalm 37:23, 24.

What is defeat? Nothing but education; nothing but the first step to something better.

—Wendell Phillips

Depression

A mental condition, emotionally or physically induced,
that renders one almost lost in periods of gloom.

"Nevertheless God, that comforteth those that are cast
down, comforted us by the coming of Titus; And not by his
coming only, but by the consolation wherewith he was comforted in you, when he told us your earnest desire, your
mourning, your fervent mind toward me; so that I rejoiced
the more."—II Corinthians 7:6,7.

"Be merciful unto me, O God, be merciful unto me: for
my soul trusteth in thee: yea, in the shadow of thy wings will
I make my refuge, until these calamities be overpast."—
Psalm 57:1.

"Heaviness in the heart of man maketh it stoop: but a
good word maketh it glad."—Proverbs 12:25.

"Casting all your care upon him; for he careth for you."—
I Peter 5:7.

"He that dwelleth in the secret place of the most High
shall abide under the shadow of the Almighty. I will say of
the LORD, He is my refuge and my fortress: my God; in him
will I trust."—Psalm 91:1,2.

"For we would not, brethren, have you ignorant of our
trouble which came to us in Asia, that we were pressed out
of measure, above strength, insomuch that we despaired
even of life: But we had the sentence of death in ourselves,
that we should not trust in ourselves, but in God which
raiseth the dead: Who delivered us from so great a death,
and doth deliver: in whom we trust that he will yet deliver
us."—II Corinthians 1:8–10.

41

"Why art thou cast down, O my soul? and why art thou disquieted within me? hope thou in God: for I shall yet praise him, who is the health of my countenance, and my God."—Psalm 42:11.

"Thou wilt keep him in perfect peace, whose mind is stayed on thee: because he trusteth in thee."—Isaiah 26:3.

"He giveth power to the faint; and to them that have no might he increaseth strength."—Isaiah 40:29.

"Then he said unto them, Go your way, eat the fat, and drink the sweet, and send portions unto them for whom nothing is prepared: for this day is holy unto our Lord: neither be ye sorry; for the joy of the LORD is your strength."—Nehemiah 8:10.

"Peace I leave with you, my peace I give unto you: not as the world giveth, give I unto you. Let not your heart be troubled, neither let it be afraid."—John 14:27.

When down in the mouth, remember Jonah. He came out all right.

–Thomas A. Edison

(Years after Edison's death, his desk was opened and the above was found on a card among his papers.)

DETERMINATION

That inner drive that almost always assures success.

"*For I determined not to know any thing among you, save Jesus Christ, and him crucified.*"—I Corinthians 2:2.

"*Our heart is not turned back, neither have our steps declined from thy way; Though thou hast sore broken us in the place of dragons, and covered us with the shadow of death.*"—Psalm 44:18,19.

"*A wise man is strong; yea, a man of knowledge increaseth strength. For by wise counsel thou shalt make thy war: and in multitude of counsellors there is safety.*"—Proverbs 24:5,6.

"*With my whole heart have I sought thee: O let me not wander from thy commandments.*"—Psalm 119:10.

"*For in him we live, and move, and have our being; as certain also of your own poets have said, For we are also his offspring.*"—Acts 17:28.

"*The thoughts of the diligent tend only to plenteousness; but of every one that is hasty only to want.*"—Proverbs 21:5.

"*For the Lord GOD will help me; therefore shall I not be confounded: therefore have I set my face like a flint, and I know that I shall not be ashamed.*"—Isaiah 50:7.

"*Strengthened with all might, according to his glorious power, unto all patience and longsuffering with joyfulness.*"—Colossians 1:11.

"Search me, O God, and know my heart: try me, and know my thoughts: And see if there be any wicked way in me, and lead me in the way everlasting." — Psalm 139:23, 24.

"Better is it that thou shouldest not vow, than that thou shouldest vow and not pay." — Ecclesiastes 5:5.

"For which of you, intending to build a tower, sitteth not down first, and counteth the cost, whether he have sufficient to finish it? Lest haply, after he hath laid the foundation, and is not able to finish it, all that behold it begin to mock him, Saying, This man began to build, and was not able to finish." — Luke 14:28–30.

"Know ye not that they which run in a race run all, but one receiveth the prize? So run, that ye may obtain." — I Corinthians 9:24.

I am only one, but still I am one. I cannot do everything, but still I can do something. And because I cannot do everything, I will not refuse to do the something that I can do; and what I can do, I ought to do; and what I ought to do, by the grace of God I will do.

—Edward Everett Hale

DISCIPLINE

Children encounter it from parents or others in authority, while adults provide it for themselves. If it is not learned and practiced, unhappiness and a lack of productivity is experienced.

"He becometh poor that dealeth with a slack hand: but the hand of the diligent maketh rich."—Proverbs 10:4.

"He that diligently seeketh good procureth favour: but he that seeketh mischief, it shall come unto him."—Proverbs 11:27.

"A servant will not be corrected by words: for though he understand he will not answer."—Proverbs 29:19.

"But I keep under my body, and bring it into subjection: lest that by any means, when I have preached to others, I myself should be a castaway."—I Corinthians 9:27.

"Let no man despise thy youth; but be thou an example of the believers, in word, in conversation, in charity, in spirit, in faith, in purity."—I Timothy 4:12.

"Take heed unto thyself, and unto the doctrine; continue in them: for in doing this thou shalt both save thyself, and them that hear thee."—I Timothy 4:16.

"The rod and reproof give wisdom: but a child left to himself bringeth his mother to shame."—Proverbs 29:15.

"Study to shew thyself approved unto God, a workman that needeth not to be ashamed, rightly dividing the word of truth."—II Timothy 2:15.

"He that spareth his rod hateth his son: but he that loveth him chasteneth him betimes."—Proverbs 13:24.

"He openeth also their ear to discipline, and commandeth that they return from iniquity."—Job 36:10.

"I will praise thee with uprightness of heart, when I shall have learned thy righteous judgments. I will keep thy statutes: O forsake me not utterly."—Psalm 119:7, 8.

"Thy word have I hid in mine heart, that I might not sin against thee."—Psalm 119:11.

"I will meditate in thy precepts, and have respect unto thy ways. I will delight myself in thy statutes: I will not forget thy word."—Psalm 119:15, 16.

"For I have kept the ways of the LORD, and have not wickedly departed from my God. For all his judgments were before me, and I did not put away his statutes from me. I was also upright before him, and I kept myself from mine iniquity."—Psalm 18:21–23.

**He who lives without discipline is
exposed to grievous ruin.**

–Thomas à Kempis

DISCOURAGEMENT

There are two kinds of people in the world: (1) the kind that
work and get what they want and (2) the kind that wring
their hands and lose what they have. There's no cure for
the first apart from success, and there is no cure
at all for the second, apart from the Bible.

*"Behold, the LORD thy God hath set the land before thee:
go up and possess it, as the LORD God of thy fathers hath
said unto thee; fear not, neither be discouraged."*—
Deuteronomy 1:21.

*"We are troubled on every side, yet not distressed; we are
perplexed, but not in despair."*—II Corinthians 4:8.

*"Knowing that he which raised up the Lord Jesus shall
raise up us also by Jesus, and shall present us with you."*—
II Corinthians 4:14.

*"A merry heart doeth good like a medicine: but a broken
spirit drieth the bones."*—Proverbs 17:22.

*"But they that wait upon the LORD shall renew their
strength; they shall mount up with wings as eagles; they
shall run, and not be weary; and they shall walk, and not
faint."*—Isaiah 40:31.

*"Have not I commanded thee? Be strong and of a good
courage; be not afraid, neither be thou dismayed: for the
LORD thy God is with thee whithersoever thou goest."*—
Joshua 1:9.

*"He healeth the broken in heart, and bindeth up their
wounds."*—Psalm 147:3.

GET A GRIP!

"But now thus saith the LORD that created thee, O Jacob, and he that formed thee, O Israel, Fear not: for I have redeemed thee, I have called thee by thy name; thou art mine."—Isaiah 43:1.

"Fear thou not; for I am with thee: be not dismayed; for I am thy God: I will strengthen thee; yea, I will help thee; yea, I will uphold thee with the right hand of my righteousness."—Isaiah 41:10.

"Come unto me, all ye that labour and are heavy laden, and I will give you rest. Take my yoke upon you, and learn of me; for I am meek and lowly in heart: and ye shall find rest unto your souls. For my yoke is easy, and my burden is light."—Matthew 11:28–30.

"For I the LORD thy God will hold thy right hand, saying unto thee, Fear not; I will help thee."—Isaiah 41:13.

"Finally, brethren, whatsoever things are true, whatsoever things are honest, whatsoever things are just, whatsoever things are pure, whatsoever things are lovely, whatsoever things are of good report; if there be any virtue, and if there be any praise, think on these things."—Philippians 4:8.

Discouragement is dissatisfaction with the past, distaste for the present, and distrust of the future. It is ingratitude for the blessings of yesterday, indifference for the opportunities of today, and insecurity regarding strength for tomorrow.

—William A. Ward

Drug Abuse

Using mind-altering substances.

"*But every man is tempted, when he is drawn away of his own lust, and enticed. Then when lust hath conceived, it bringeth forth sin: and sin, when it is finished, bringeth forth death.*"—James 1:14,15.

"*For God hath not given us the spirit of fear; but of power, and of love, and of a sound mind.*"—II Timothy 1:7.

"*For the time past of our life may suffice us to have wrought the will of the Gentiles, when we walked in lasciviousness, lusts, excess of wine, revellings, banquetings, and abominable idolatries.*"—I Peter 4:3.

"*And ye shall know the truth, and the truth shall make you free.*"
"*If the Son therefore shall make you free, ye shall be free indeed.*"—John 8:32,36.

"*There hath no temptation taken you but such as is common to man: but God is faithful, who will not suffer you to be tempted above that ye are able; but will with the temptation also make a way to escape, that ye may be able to bear it.*"—I Corinthians 10:13.

"*Now the works of the flesh are manifest, which are these; Adultery, fornication, uncleanness, lasciviousness, Idolatry, witchcraft, hatred, variance, emulations, wrath, strife, seditions, heresies, Envyings, murders, drunkenness, revellings, and such like: of the which I tell you before, as I have also told you in time past, that they which do such things shall not inherit the kingdom of God.*"—Galatians 5:19–21.

"What? know ye not that your body is the temple of the Holy Ghost which is in you, which ye have of God, and ye are not your own? For ye are bought with a price: therefore glorify God in your body, and in your spirit, which are God's."—I Corinthians 6:19,20.

"I beseech you therefore, brethren, by the mercies of God, that ye present your bodies a living sacrifice, holy, acceptable unto God, which is your reasonable service. And be not conformed to this world: but be ye transformed by the renewing of your mind, that ye may prove what is that good, and acceptable, and perfect, will of God."—Romans 12:1,2.

"Love not the world, neither the things that are in the world. If any man love the world, the love of the Father is not in him. For all that is in the world, the lust of the flesh, and the lust of the eyes, and the pride of life, is not of the Father, but is of the world. And the world passeth away, and the lust thereof: but he that doeth the will of God abideth for ever."—I John 2:15–17.

"Therefore, brethren, we are debtors, not to the flesh, to live after the flesh. For if ye live after the flesh, ye shall die: but if ye through the Spirit do mortify the deeds of the body, ye shall live."—Romans 8:12,13.

"And they that are Christ's have crucified the flesh with the affections and lusts."—Galatians 5:24.

There is no doubt about it. Almost every drug addict I've talked to said he started with marijuana.

—Chief John Enright
Federal Bureau of
Narcotics and Dangerous
Drugs

50

ETERNAL LIFE

**The wonderful aspect of life in Christ
is that it is everlasting.**

"And this is the record, that God hath given to us eternal life, and this life is in his Son. He that hath the Son hath life; and he that hath not the Son of God hath not life. These things have I written unto you that believe on the name of the Son of God; that ye may know that ye have eternal life, and that ye may believe on the name of the Son of God."—I John 5:11–13.

"Verily, verily, I say unto you, He that believeth on me hath everlasting life."—John 6:47.

"For since by man came death, by man came also the resurrection of the dead."—I Corinthians 15:21.

"For the Lord himself shall descend from heaven with a shout, with the voice of the archangel, and with the trump of God: and the dead in Christ shall rise first."—I Thessalonians 4:16.

"For God so loved the world, that he gave his only begotten Son, that whosoever believeth in him should not perish, but have everlasting life."—John 3:16.

"For he that soweth to his flesh shall of the flesh reap corruption; but he that soweth to the Spirit shall of the Spirit reap life everlasting."—Galatians 6:8.

"For the wages of sin is death; but the gift of God is eternal life through Jesus Christ our Lord."—Romans 6:23.

"*And many of them that sleep in the dust of the earth shall awake, some to everlasting life, and some to shame and everlasting contempt.*"—Daniel 12:2.

"*But is now made manifest by the appearing of our Saviour Jesus Christ, who hath abolished death, and hath brought life and immortality to light through the gospel.*"—II Timothy 1:10.

"*For we know that if our earthly house of this tabernacle were dissolved, we have a building of God, an house not made with hands, eternal in the heavens.*"—II Corinthians 5:1.

"*In my Father's house are many mansions: if it were not so, I would have told you. I go to prepare a place for you. And if I go and prepare a place for you, I will come again, and receive you unto myself; that where I am, there ye may be also.*"—John 14:2,3.

"*My sheep hear my voice, and I know them, and they follow me: And I give unto them eternal life; and they shall never perish, neither shall any man pluck them out of my hand.*"—John 10:27,28.

The truest end of life is to know the life that never ends.

–William Penn

EXAMPLE

To live in such a manner that if others lived
just like you they would be fine.

*"Let no man despise thy youth; but be thou an example of
the believers, in word, in conversation, in charity, in spirit,
in faith, in purity."*—I Timothy 4:12.

*"For even hereunto were ye called: because Christ also
suffered for us, leaving us an example, that ye should follow
his steps."*—I Peter 2:21.

*"For I have given you an example, that ye should do as I
have done to you."*—John 13:15.

*"Even as Sodom and Gomorrha, and the cities about
them in like manner, giving themselves over to fornication,
and going after strange flesh, are set forth for an example,
suffering the vengeance of eternal fire."*—Jude 7.

*"Now these things were our examples, to the intent we
should not lust after evil things, as they also lusted."*—
I Corinthians 10:6.

*"Let us labour therefore to enter into that rest, lest any
man fall after the same example of unbelief."*—Hebrews 4:11.

*"My son, be wise, and make my heart glad, that I may
answer him that reproacheth me."*—Proverbs 27:11.

*"No man, when he hath lighted a candle, putteth it in a
secret place, neither under a bushel, but on a candlestick,
that they which come in may see the light."*—Luke 11:33.

"Be ye followers of me, even as I also am of Christ."—
I Corinthians 11:1.

"For our rejoicing is this, the testimony of our conscience, that in simplicity and godly sincerity, not with fleshly wisdom, but by the grace of God, we have had our conversation in the world, and more abundantly to you-ward."—
II Corinthians 1:12.

"And grieve not the holy Spirit of God, whereby ye are sealed unto the day of redemption. Let all bitterness, and wrath, and anger, and clamour, and evil speaking, be put away from you, with all malice: And be ye kind one to another, tenderhearted, forgiving one another, even as God for Christ's sake hath forgiven you. Be ye therefore followers of God, as dear children; And walk in love, as Christ also hath loved us, and hath given himself for us an offering and a sacrifice to God for a sweetsmelling savour."—Ephesians 4:30–5:2.

Example is the school of mankind, and they will learn at no other.

−Edmund Burke

Example is always more efficacious than precept.

−Samuel Johnson

FAILURE

It is only true failure when you don't learn from it.

"The LORD is my rock, and my fortress, and my deliverer; my God, my strength, in whom I will trust; my buckler, and the horn of my salvation, and my high tower. I will call upon the LORD, who is worthy to be praised: so shall I be saved from mine enemies."—Psalm 18:2,3.

"The LORD is good, a strong hold in the day of trouble; and he knoweth them that trust in him."—Nahum 1:7.

"We are troubled on every side, yet not distressed; we are perplexed, but not in despair; Persecuted, but not forsaken; cast down, but not destroyed."—II Corinthians 4:8,9.

"Let them be confounded that persecute me, but let not me be confounded: let them be dismayed, but let not me be dismayed: bring upon them the day of evil, and destroy them with double destruction."—Jeremiah 17:18.

"Though I walk in the midst of trouble, thou wilt revive me: thou shalt stretch forth thine hand against the wrath of mine enemies, and thy right hand shall save me."—Psalm 138:7.

"Let not your heart be troubled: ye believe in God, believe also in me."—John 14:1.

"When thou passest through the waters, I will be with thee; and through the rivers, they shall not overflow thee: when thou walkest through the fire, thou shalt not be burned; neither shall the flame kindle upon thee."—Isaiah 43:2.

"And we know that all things work together for good to them that love God, to them who are the called according to his purpose."—Romans 8:28.

"I will be glad and rejoice in thy mercy: for thou hast considered my trouble; thou hast known my soul in adversities."—Psalm 31:7.

"I will lift up mine eyes unto the hills, from whence cometh my help. My help cometh from the LORD, which made heaven and earth."—Psalm 121:1,2.

"For we have not an high priest which cannot be touched with the feeling of our infirmities; but was in all points tempted like as we are, yet without sin. Let us therefore come boldly unto the throne of grace, that we may obtain mercy, and find grace to help in time of need."—Hebrews 4:15,16.

"Casting all your care upon him; for he careth for you."—I Peter 5:7.

"Be careful for nothing; but in every thing by prayer and supplication with thanksgiving let your requests be made known unto God. And the peace of God, which passeth all understanding, shall keep your hearts and minds through Christ Jesus."—Philippians 4:6,7.

"Therefore the redeemed of the LORD shall return, and come with singing unto Zion; and everlasting joy shall be upon their head: they shall obtain gladness and joy; and sorrow and mourning shall flee away."—Isaiah 51:11.

Failure should be our teacher, not our undertaker. Failure is delay, not defeat. It is a temporary detour, not a dead end.

—Denis Waitley

FRIENDS

The few people who love and accept you, and who
will be honest with you, no matter what.

"A friend loveth at all times, and a brother is born for
adversity." — Proverbs 17:17.

"A man that hath friends must shew himself friendly:
and there is a friend that sticketh closer than a brother." —
Proverbs 18:24.

"A froward man soweth strife: and a whisperer separateth chief friends." — Proverbs 16:28.

"Greater love hath no man than this, that a man lay
down his life for his friends. Ye are my friends, if ye do whatsoever I command you. Henceforth I call you not servants;
for the servant knoweth not what his lord doeth: but I have
called you friends; for all things that I have heard of my
Father I have made known unto you." — John 15:13–15.

"And the scripture was fulfilled which saith, Abraham
believed God, and it was imputed unto him for righteousness: and he was called the Friend of God." — James 2:23.

"He that walketh with wise men shall be wise: but a
companion of fools shall be destroyed." — Proverbs 13:20.

"Ye adulterers and adulteresses, know ye not that the
friendship of the world is enmity with God? whosoever
therefore will be a friend of the world is the enemy of
God." — James 4:4.

"Can two walk together, except they be agreed?" — Amos 3:3.

"Bear ye one another's burdens, and so fulfil the law of Christ."—Galatians 6:2.

"Faithful are the wounds of a friend; but the kisses of an enemy are deceitful."—Proverbs 27:6.

"For if they fall, the one will lift up his fellow: but woe to him that is alone when he falleth; for he hath not another to help him up."—Ecclesiastes 4:10.

"Thine own friend, and thy father's friend, forsake not; neither go into thy brother's house in the day of thy calamity: for better is a neighbour that is near than a brother far off."—Proverbs 27:10.

"Finally, be ye all of one mind, having compassion one of another, love as brethren, be pitiful, be courteous: Not rendering evil for evil, or railing for railing: but contrariwise blessing; knowing that ye are thereunto called, that ye should inherit a blessing."—I Peter 3:8,9.

Friendship improves happiness and abates misery by the doubling our joy and the dividing our grief.

—Joseph Addison

FUTURE

All of those opportunities that lie ahead.

"My son, forget not my law; but let thine heart keep my commandments: For length of days, and long life, and peace, shall they add to thee."—Proverbs 3:1,2.

"And the world passeth away, and the lust thereof: but he that doeth the will of God abideth for ever."—I John 2:17.

"A man's heart deviseth his way: but the LORD directeth his steps."—Proverbs 16:9.

"Let thine eyes look right on, and let thine eyelids look straight before thee. Ponder the path of thy feet, and let all thy ways be established."—Proverbs 4:25,26.

"Commit thy works unto the LORD, and thy thoughts shall be established."—Proverbs 16:3.

"Jesus said unto him, If thou canst believe, all things are possible to him that believeth."—Mark 9:23.

"Fret not thyself because of evil men, neither be thou envious at the wicked; For there shall be no reward to the evil man; the candle of the wicked shall be put out."—Proverbs 24:19,20.

"For I know the thoughts that I think toward you, saith the LORD, thoughts of peace, and not of evil, to give you an expected end."—Jeremiah 29:11.

"Let not thine heart envy sinners: but be thou in the fear of the LORD all the day long. For surely there is an end; and thine expectation shall not be cut off."—Proverbs 23:17,18.

59

"Without counsel purposes are disappointed: but in the multitude of counsellors they are established."—Proverbs 15:22.

"Whereas ye know not what shall be on the morrow. For what is your life? It is even a vapour, that appeareth for a little time, and then vanisheth away."—James 4:14.

"But as it is written, Eye hath not seen, nor ear heard, neither have entered into the heart of man, the things which God hath prepared for them that love him."—I Corinthians 2:9.

"And Joshua said unto the people, Sanctify yourselves: for to morrow the LORD will do wonders among you."—Joshua 3:5.

"Boast not thyself of to morrow; for thou knowest not what a day may bring forth."—Proverbs 27:1.

The best thing about the future is that it comes only one day at a time.
—Abraham Lincoln

GENEROSITY

The wonderful characteristic of sensing the needs
of others and responding positively.

"Speak unto the children of Israel, that they bring me an
offering: of every man that giveth it willingly with his heart
ye shall take my offering."—Exodus 25:2.

"The desire of the slothful killeth him; for his hands
refuse to labour. He coveteth greedily all the day long: but
the righteous giveth and spareth not."—Proverbs 21:25, 26.

"He is ever merciful, and lendeth; and his seed is
blessed."—Psalm 37:26.

"Give to him that asketh thee, and from him that would
borrow of thee turn not thou away."—Matthew 5:42.

"There is that scattereth, and yet increaseth; and there is
that withholdeth more than is meet, but it tendeth to poverty.
The liberal soul shall be made fat: and he that watereth
shall be watered also himself."—Proverbs 11:24, 25.

"Take heed that ye do not your alms before men, to be seen
of them: otherwise ye have no reward of your Father which
is in heaven."—Matthew 6:1.

"He that hath a bountiful eye shall be blessed; for he
giveth of his bread to the poor."—Proverbs 22:9.

"But this I say, He which soweth sparingly shall reap also
sparingly; and he which soweth bountifully shall reap also
bountifully. Every man according as he purposeth in his
heart, so let him give; not grudgingly, or of necessity: for God
loveth a cheerful giver."—II Corinthians 9:6, 7.

61

"Withhold not good from them to whom it is due, when it is in the power of thine hand to do it."—Proverbs 3:27.

"Therefore, as ye abound in every thing, in faith, and utterance, and knowledge, and in all diligence, and in your love to us, see that ye abound in this grace also."— II Corinthians 8:7.

"How that in a great trial of affliction the abundance of their joy and their deep poverty abounded unto the riches of their liberality."—II Corinthians 8:2.

"And whosoever shall give to drink unto one of these little ones a cup of cold water only in the name of a disciple, verily I say unto you, he shall in no wise lose his reward."— Matthew 10:42.

Generosity is a matter of the heart and not the pocketbook.

—Fred P. Carson

You can give without loving, but you can never love without giving.

—Robert Louis Stevenson

GOALS

Setting reachable rungs on the ladder of success.
Long- or short-term, they are important, but
the short-term ones are more important.

"Let thine eyes look right on, and let thine eyelids look straight before thee. Ponder the path of thy feet, and let all thy ways be established. Turn not to the right hand nor to the left: remove thy foot from evil."—Proverbs 4:25–27.

"Wherefore we labour, that, whether present or absent, we may be accepted of him."—II Corinthians 5:9.

"I therefore so run, not as uncertainly; so fight I, not as one that beateth the air."—I Corinthians 9:26.

"And let us not be weary in well doing: for in due season we shall reap, if we faint not."—Galatians 6:9.

"Now the end of the commandment is charity out of a pure heart, and of a good conscience, and of faith unfeigned."—I Timothy 1:5.

"The thoughts of the diligent tend only to plenteousness; but of every one that is hasty only to want."—Proverbs 21:5.

"See then that ye walk circumspectly, not as fools, but as wise, Redeeming the time, because the days are evil."—Ephesians 5:15, 16.

"My son, let not them depart from thine eyes: keep sound wisdom and discretion: So shall they be life unto thy soul, and grace to thy neck."—Proverbs 3:21, 22.

GET A GRIP!

"He that gathereth in summer is a wise son: but he that sleepeth in harvest is a son that causeth shame."— Proverbs 10:5.

"Delight thyself also in the LORD; *and he shall give thee the desires of thine heart. Commit thy way unto the* LORD; *trust also in him; and he shall bring it to pass."*— Psalm 37:4,5.

"The preparations of the heart in man, and the answer of the tongue, is from the LORD."—Proverbs 16:1.

"Walk in wisdom toward them that are without, redeeming the time."—Colossians 4:5.

"I press toward the mark for the prize of the high calling of God in Christ Jesus."—Philippians 3:14.

Obstacles are those frightful things you see when you take your eyes off your goal.

−Henry Ford

GRATITUDE

Thankfulness is something that we learn, not something we are born with. If we don't learn it, we become loathsome indeed.

"O give thanks unto the LORD; for he is good; for his mercy endureth for ever."—I Chronicles 16:34.

"Make a joyful noise unto the LORD, all ye lands. Serve the LORD with gladness: come before his presence with singing. Know ye that the LORD he is God: it is he that hath made us, and not we ourselves; we are his people, and the sheep of his pasture. Enter into his gates with thanksgiving, and into his courts with praise: be thankful unto him, and bless his name. For the LORD is good; his mercy is everlasting; and his truth endureth to all generations."— Psalm 100.

"But thanks be to God, which giveth us the victory through our Lord Jesus Christ."—I Corinthians 15:57.

"O come, let us sing unto the LORD: let us make a joyful noise to the rock of our salvation. Let us come before his presence with thanksgiving, and make a joyful noise unto him with psalms."—Psalm 95:1,2.

"For every creature of God is good, and nothing to be refused, if it be received with thanksgiving."—I Timothy 4:4.

"And whatsoever ye do in word or deed, do all in the name of the Lord Jesus, giving thanks to God and the Father by him."—Colossians 3:17.

"O give thanks unto the LORD; for he is good: for his mercy endureth for ever."—Psalm 136:1.

65

GET A GRIP!

"It is a good thing to give thanks unto the LORD, and to sing praises unto thy name, O most High: To shew forth thy lovingkindness in the morning, and thy faithfulness every night." —Psalm 92:1, 2.

"He that regardeth the day, regardeth it unto the Lord; and he that regardeth not the day, to the Lord he doth not regard it. He that eateth, eateth to the Lord, for he giveth God thanks; and he that eateth not, to the Lord he eateth not, and giveth God thanks." —Romans 14:6.

"O give thanks unto the LORD, for he is good: for his mercy endureth for ever. Let the redeemed of the LORD say so, whom he hath redeemed from the hand of the enemy." —Psalm 107:1, 2.

"And I thank Christ Jesus our Lord, who hath enabled me, for that he counted me faithful, putting me into the ministry." —I Timothy 1:12.

"Be careful for nothing; but in every thing by prayer and supplication with thanksgiving let your requests be made known unto God. And the peace of God, which passeth all understanding, shall keep your hearts and minds through Christ Jesus." —Philippians 4:6, 7.

"And offer a sacrifice of thanksgiving with leaven, and proclaim and publish the free offerings: for this liketh you, O ye children of Israel, saith the Lord GOD." —Amos 4:5.

"Continue in prayer, and watch in the same with thanksgiving." —Colossians 4:2.

He who forgets the language of gratitude is not likely to be on speaking terms with God.

HAPPINESS

An inner joy that cannot be secured with money or things. Oftentimes it is a simple choice. True faith in Christ and his keeping power can be a terrific source of happiness.

"This day is holy unto our Lord: neither be ye sorry; for the joy of the LORD is your strength."—Nehemiah 8:10.

"Delight thyself also in the LORD; and he shall give thee the desires of thine heart."—Psalm 37:4.

"Thou lovest righteousness, and hatest wickedness: therefore God, thy God, hath anointed thee with the oil of gladness above thy fellows."—Psalm 45:7.

"The desire of the righteous is only good: but the expectation of the wicked is wrath."—Proverbs 11:23.

"Light is sown for the righteous, and gladness for the upright in heart."—Psalm 97:11.

"Serve the LORD with gladness: come before his presence with singing. Know ye that the LORD he is God: it is he that hath made us, and not we ourselves; we are his people, and the sheep of his pasture."—Psalm 100:2,3.

"Who redeemeth thy life from destruction; who crowneth thee with lovingkindness and tender mercies; Who satisfieth thy mouth with good things; so that thy youth is renewed like the eagle's."—Psalm 103:4,5.

"Thy testimonies also are my delight and my counsellors."—Psalm 119:24.

"*Happy is the man that findeth wisdom, and the man that getteth understanding.*"

"*Her ways are ways of pleasantness, and all her paths are peace. She is a tree of life to them that lay hold upon her: and happy is every one that retaineth her.*"—Proverbs 3:13, 17, 18.

"*For thou shalt eat the labour of thine hands: happy shalt thou be, and it shall be well with thee.*"—Psalm 128:2.

"*Whom having not seen, ye love; in whom, though now ye see him not, yet believing, ye rejoice with joy unspeakable and full of glory: Receiving the end of your faith, even the salvation of your souls.*"—I Peter 1:8, 9.

"*For I rejoiced greatly, when the brethren came and testified of the truth that is in thee, even as thou walkest in the truth. I have no greater joy than to hear that my children walk in truth.*"—III John 3, 4.

"*Now unto him that is able to keep you from falling, and to present you faultless before the presence of his glory with exceeding joy, To the only wise God our Saviour, be glory and majesty, dominion and power, both now and ever. Amen.*"—Jude 24, 25.

One of the most miserable people in all of the world is the person who spends every waking hour trying to find something that will make "me" happy.

—Lindsay Terry

HEAVEN

The eternal home with the Heavenly Father of all
who have accepted Christ as Saviour.

"For Christ is not entered into the holy places made with hands, which are the figures of the true; but into heaven itself, now to appear in the presence of God for us."— Hebrews 9:24.

"And I saw no temple therein: for the Lord God Almighty and the Lamb are the temple of it. And the city had no need of the sun, neither of the moon, to shine in it: for the glory of God did lighten it, and the Lamb is the light thereof. And the nations of them which are saved shall walk in the light of it: and the kings of the earth do bring their glory and honour into it."—Revelation 21:22–24.

"But now they desire a better country, that is, an heavenly: wherefore God is not ashamed to be called their God: for he hath prepared for them a city."—Hebrews 11:16.

"But ye are come unto mount Sion, and unto the city of the living God, the heavenly Jerusalem, and to an innumerable company of angels."—Hebrews 12:22.

"Beloved, now are we the sons of God, and it doth not yet appear what we shall be: but we know that, when he shall appear, we shall be like him; for we shall see him as he is."— I John 3:2.

"And I say unto you, That many shall come from the east and west, and shall sit down with Abraham, and Isaac, and Jacob, in the kingdom of heaven."—Matthew 8:11.

69

"After this I beheld, and, lo, a great multitude, which no man could number, of all nations, and kindreds, and people, and tongues, stood before the throne, and before the Lamb, clothed with white robes, and palms in their hands."— Revelation 7:9.

"And they sing the song of Moses the servant of God, and the song of the Lamb, saying, Great and marvellous are thy works, Lord God Almighty; just and true are thy ways, thou King of saints."—Revelation 15:3.

"And God shall wipe away all tears from their eyes; and there shall be no more death, neither sorrow, nor crying, neither shall there be any more pain: for the former things are passed away."—Revelation 21:4.

"For our conversation is in heaven; from whence also we look for the Saviour, the Lord Jesus Christ."—Philippians 3:20.

"In my Father's house are many mansions: if it were not so, I would have told you. I go to prepare a place for you. And if I go and prepare a place for you, I will come again, and receive you unto myself; that where I am, there ye may be also."—John 14:2,3.

"And no man hath ascended up to heaven, but he that came down from heaven, even the Son of man which is in heaven."—John 3:13.

He who is on the road to Heaven should not be content to go there alone.

–Unknown

HELL

A place of eternal punishment and separation from God.

"And fear not them which kill the body, but are not able to kill the soul: but rather fear him which is able to destroy both soul and body in hell."—Matthew 10:28.

"And cast ye the unprofitable servant into outer darkness: there shall be weeping and gnashing of teeth."—Matthew 25:30.

"And I say also unto thee, That thou art Peter, and upon this rock I will build my church; and the gates of hell shall not prevail against it."—Matthew 16:18.

"For if God spared not the angels that sinned, but cast them down to hell, and delivered them into chains of darkness, to be reserved unto judgment."—II Peter 2:4.

"The wicked shall be turned into hell, and all the nations that forget God."—Psalm 9:17.

"Stolen waters are sweet, and bread eaten in secret is pleasant. But he knoweth not that the dead are there; and that her guests are in the depths of hell."—Proverbs 9:17,18.

"Enter ye in at the strait gate: for wide is the gate, and broad is the way, that leadeth to destruction, and many there be which go in thereat."—Matthew 7:13.

"For God so loved the world, that he gave his only begotten Son, that whosoever believeth in him should not perish, but have everlasting life."—John 3:16.

71

"How shall we escape, if we neglect so great salvation; which at the first began to be spoken by the Lord, and was confirmed unto us by them that heard him."—Hebrews 2:3.

"And I say unto you my friends, Be not afraid of them that kill the body, and after that have no more that they can do. But I will forewarn you whom ye shall fear: Fear him, which after he hath killed hath power to cast into hell; yea, I say unto you, Fear him."—Luke 12:4,5.

"And the beast was taken, and with him the false prophet that wrought miracles before him, with which he deceived them that had received the mark of the beast, and them that worshipped his image. These both were cast alive into a lake of fire burning with brimstone."—Revelation 19:20.

"For the wages of sin is death; but the gift of God is eternal life through Jesus Christ our Lord."—Romans 6:23.

"I tell you, Nay: but, except ye repent, ye shall all likewise perish."—Luke 13:3.

**The safest road to hell is the gradual one—
the gentle slope, soft underfoot, without
sudden turnings, without milestones,
without signposts.**

–C. S. Lewis

HOLY BIBLE

Our God-breathed book; the verbally inspired,
eternal, inerrant Word of God

"And that from a child thou hast known the holy scriptures, which are able to make thee wise unto salvation through faith which is in Christ Jesus. All scripture is given by inspiration of God, and is profitable for doctrine, for reproof, for correction, for instruction in righteousness."—II Timothy 3:15,16.

"For ever, O LORD, thy word is settled in heaven."—Psalm 119:89.

"Concerning thy testimonies, I have known of old that Thou hast founded them for ever."—Psalm 119:152.

"Thy word is true from the beginning: and every one of thy righteous judgments endureth for ever."—Psalm 119:160.

"The law of the LORD is perfect, converting the soul: the testimony of the LORD is sure, making wise the simple."—Psalm 19:7.

"The grass withereth, the flower fadeth: but the word of our God shall stand for ever."—Isaiah 40:8.

"Being born again, not of corruptible seed, but of incorruptible, by the word of God, which liveth and abideth for ever. For all flesh is as grass, and all the glory of man as the flower of grass. The grass withereth, and the flower thereof falleth away: But the word of the Lord endureth for ever. And this is the word which by the gospel is preached unto you."—I Peter 1:23–25.

"For the prophecy came not in old time by the will of man: but holy men of God spake as they were moved by the Holy Ghost."—II Peter 1:21.

"Every word of God is pure: he is a shield unto them that put their trust in him."—Proverbs 30:5.

"But he answered and said, It is written, Man shall not live by bread alone, but by every word that proceedeth out of the mouth of God."—Matthew 4:4.

"For the word of God is quick, and powerful, and sharper than any twoedged sword, piercing even to the dividing asunder of soul and spirit, and of the joints and marrow, and is a discerner of the thoughts and intents of the heart."—Hebrews 4:12.

"Thy word have I hid in mine heart, that I might not sin against thee."—Psalm 119:11.

"Study to shew thyself approved unto God, a workman that needeth not to be ashamed, rightly dividing the word of truth."—II Timothy 2:15.

"Which things also we speak, not in the words which man's wisdom teacheth, but which the Holy Ghost teacheth; comparing spiritual things with spiritual."—I Corinthians 2:13.

Nothing any man can say or think about the Bible is as important as what the Bible says about itself.

—John R. Rice

HOME

The place where, when you have to go there,
they have to take you in. —Robert Frost

"Better is a dry morsel, and quietness therewith, than an house full of sacrifices with strife." —Proverbs 17:1.

"Children, obey your parents in the Lord: for this is right. Honour thy father and mother; which is the first commandment with promise; That it may be well with thee, and thou mayest live long on the earth." —Ephesians 6:1–3.

"And these words, which I command thee this day, shall be in thine heart: And thou shalt teach them diligently unto thy children, and shalt talk of them when thou sittest in thine house, and when thou walkest by the way, and when thou liest down, and when thou risest up." — Deuteronomy 6:6,7.

"And if it seem evil unto you to serve the LORD, choose you this day whom ye will serve; whether the gods which your fathers served that were on the other side of the flood, or the gods of the Amorites, in whose land ye dwell: but as for me and my house, we will serve the LORD." —Joshua 24:15.

"And, ye fathers, provoke not your children to wrath: but bring them up in the nurture and admonition of the Lord." —Ephesians 6:4.

"Train up a child in the way he should go: and when he is old, he will not depart from it." —Proverbs 22:6.

"Honour thy father and thy mother: that thy days may be long upon the land which the LORD thy God giveth thee." — Exodus 20:12.

75

"Lo, children are an heritage of the LORD: and the fruit of the womb is his reward. As arrows are in the hand of a mighty man; so are children of the youth."—Psalm 127:3,4.

"And he shall turn the heart of the fathers to the children, and the heart of the children to their fathers, lest I come and smite the earth with a curse."—Malachi 4:6.

"Children's children are the crown of old men; and the glory of children are their fathers."—Proverbs 17:6.

"But if any widow have children or nephews, let them learn first to shew piety at home, and to requite their parents: for that is good and acceptable before God."—I Timothy 5:4.

"To be discreet, chaste, keepers at home, good, obedient to their own husbands, that the word of God be not blasphemed."—Titus 2:5.

A broken home is the world's greatest wreck.
-Unknown

HOMOSEXUALITY

Sexual activity between those of the same sex.

"If a man also lie with mankind, as he lieth with a woman, both of them have committed an abomination: they shall surely be put to death; their blood shall be upon them."—Leviticus 20:13.

"Know ye not that the unrighteous shall not inherit the kingdom of God? Be not deceived: neither fornicators, nor idolaters, nor adulterers, nor effeminate, nor abusers of themselves with mankind, Nor thieves, nor covetous, nor drunkards, nor revilers, nor extortioners, shall inherit the kingdom of God."—I Corinthians 6:9,10.

"And likewise also the men, leaving the natural use of the woman, burned in their lust one toward another; men with men working that which is unseemly, and receiving in themselves that recompence of their error which was meet. And even as they did not like to retain God in their knowledge, God gave them over to a reprobate mind, to do those things which are not convenient."—Romans 1:27,28.

"But every man is tempted, when he is drawn away of his own lust, and enticed. Then when lust hath conceived, it bringeth forth sin: and sin, when it is finished, bringeth forth death."—James 1:14,15.

"Thou shalt not lie with mankind, as with womankind: it is abomination. Neither shalt thou lie with any beast to defile thyself therewith: neither shall any woman stand before a beast to lie down thereto: it is confusion."—Leviticus 18:22,23.

GET A GRIP!

"There shall be no whore of the daughters of Israel, nor a sodomite of the sons of Israel."—Deuteronomy 23:17.

"Now as they were making their hearts merry, behold, the men of the city, certain sons of Belial, beset the house round about, and beat at the door, and spake to the master of the house, the old man, saying, Bring forth the man that came into thine house, that we may know him. And the man, the master of the house, went out unto them, and said unto them, Nay, my brethren, nay, I pray you, do not so wickedly; seeing that this man is come into mine house, do not this folly. Behold, here is my daughter a maiden, and his concubine; them I will bring out now, and humble ye them, and do with them what seemeth good unto you: but unto this man do not so vile a thing."—Judges 19:22–24.

"And they have cast lots for my people; and have given a boy for an harlot, and sold a girl for wine, that they might drink."—Joel 3:3.

"For whoremongers, for them that defile themselves with mankind, for menstealers, for liars, for perjured persons, and if there be any other thing that is contrary to sound doctrine."—I Timothy 1:10.

"And they called unto Lot, and said unto him, Where are the men which came in to thee this night? bring them out unto us, that we may know them."—Genesis 19:5.

"And there were also sodomites in the land: and they did according to all the abominations of the nations which the LORD cast out before the children of Israel."—I Kings 14:24.

No judgments will, of themselves, change the corrupt natures and purposes of wicked men.

–Matthew Henry

HONESTY

An unwillingness to be untruthful to oneself or to anyone else.

"The just man walketh in his integrity: his children are blessed after him."—Proverbs 20:7.

"Two things have I required of thee; deny me them not before I die: Remove far from me vanity and lies: give me neither poverty nor riches; feed me with food convenient for me."—Proverbs 30:7,8.

"Run ye to and fro through the streets of Jerusalem, and see now, and know, and seek in the broad places thereof, if ye can find a man, if there be any that executeth judgment, that seeketh the truth; and I will pardon it."—Jeremiah 5:1.

"But that on the good ground are they, which in an honest and good heart, having heard the word, keep it, and bring forth fruit with patience."—Luke 8:15.

"Recompense to no man evil for evil. Provide things honest in the sight of all men."—Romans 12:17.

"Providing for honest things, not only in the sight of the Lord, but also in the sight of men."—II Corinthians 8:21.

"Let us walk honestly, as in the day; not in rioting and drunkenness, not in chambering and wantonness, not in strife and envying."—Romans 13:13.

"Finally, brethren, whatsoever things are true, whatsoever things are honest, whatsoever things are just, whatsoever things are pure, whatsoever things are lovely, whatsoever things are of good report; if there be any virtue, and if there be any praise, think on these things."—Philippians 4:8.

"That ye may walk honestly toward them that are without, and that ye may have lack of nothing."— I Thessalonians 4:12.

"For kings, and for all that are in authority; that we may lead a quiet and peaceable life in all godliness and honesty."—I Timothy 2:2.

"Pray for us: for we trust we have a good conscience, in all things willing to live honestly."—Hebrews 13:18.

"A just weight and balance are the LORD'S: all the weights of the bag are his work."—Proverbs 16:11.

"Who shall ascend into the hill of the LORD? or who shall stand in his holy place? He that hath clean hands, and a pure heart; who hath not lifted up his soul unto vanity, nor sworn deceitfully."—Psalm 24:3, 4.

How desperately difficult it is to be honest with oneself. It is much easier to be honest with other people.

–Edward Benson

HONOR

That quality of life that allows one to live with himself without disdain. The reward of true integrity.

"*Before destruction the heart of man is haughty, and before honour is humility.*"—Proverbs 18:12.

"*And ye will not come to me, that ye might have life. I receive not honour from men.*"—John 5:40, 41.

"*Get wisdom, get understanding: forget it not; neither decline from the words of my mouth.*"
"*Exalt her, and she shall promote thee: she shall bring thee to honour, when thou dost embrace her.*"—Proverbs 4:5, 8.

"*And they were offended in him. But Jesus said unto them, A prophet is not without honour, save in his own country, and in his own house.*"—Matthew 13:57.

"*The fear of the LORD is the instruction of wisdom; and before honour is humility.*"—Proverbs 15:33.

"*Render therefore to all their dues: tribute to whom tribute is due; custom to whom custom; fear to whom fear; honour to whom honour.*"—Romans 13:7.

"*To execute upon them the judgment written: this honour have all his saints. Praise ye the LORD.*"—Psalm 149:9.

"*He that followeth after righteousness and mercy findeth life, righteousness, and honour.*"—Proverbs 21:21.

"*But glory, honour, and peace, to every man that worketh good, to the Jew first, and also to the Gentile.*"—Romans 2:10.

"As snow in summer, and as rain in harvest, so honour is not seemly for a fool."—Proverbs 26:1.

"A man's pride shall bring him low: but honour shall uphold the humble in spirit."—Proverbs 29:23.

"And no man taketh this honour unto himself, but he that is called of God, as was Aaron."—Hebrews 5:4.

"Jesus answered, If I honour myself, my honour is nothing: it is my Father that honoureth me; of whom ye say, that he is your God."—John 8:54.

"Strength and honour are her clothing; and she shall rejoice in time to come."—Proverbs 31:25.

"That every one of you should know how to possess his vessel in sanctification and honour."—I Thessalonians 4:4.

It is better to deserve honors and not have them than to have them and not deserve them.

–Mark Twain

INTEGRITY

Having godly character is most important, after your conversion experience. It includes honesty, fairness and faithfulness.

"My righteousness I hold fast, and will not let it go: my heart shall not reproach me so long as I live."—Job 27:6.

"Even a child is known by his doings, whether his work be pure, and whether it be right."—Proverbs 20:11.

"My brethren, count it all joy when ye fall into divers temptations; Knowing this, that the trying of your faith worketh patience. But let patience have her perfect work, that ye may be perfect and entire, wanting nothing."—James 1:2–4.

"A false balance is abomination to the LORD: but a just weight is his delight."—Proverbs 11:1.

"And herein do I exercise myself, to have always a conscience void of offence toward God, and toward men."— Acts 24:16.

"As the fining pot for silver, and the furnace for gold; so is a man to his praise."—Proverbs 27:21.

"Therefore all things whatsoever ye would that men should do to you, do ye even so to them: for this is the law and the prophets."—Matthew 7:12.

"He that walketh righteously, and speaketh uprightly; he that despiseth the gain of oppressions, that shaketh his hands from holding of bribes, that stoppeth his ears from hearing of blood, and shutteth his eyes from seeing evil."— Isaiah 33:15.

GET A GRIP!

"Thus saith the LORD; Execute ye judgment and righteousness, and deliver the spoiled out of the hand of the oppressor: and do no wrong, do no violence to the stranger, the fatherless, nor the widow, neither shed innocent blood in this place."—Jeremiah 22:3.

"The just man walketh in his integrity: his children are blessed after him."—Proverbs 20:7.

"But your iniquities have separated between you and your God, and your sins have hid his face from you, that he will not hear. For your hands are defiled with blood, and your fingers with iniquity; your lips have spoken lies, your tongue hath muttered perverseness."—Isaiah 59:2,3.

"Thou shalt destroy them that speak leasing: the LORD will abhor the bloody and deceitful man."—Psalm 5:6.

"A false witness shall not be unpunished, and he that speaketh lies shall not escape."—Proverbs 19:5.

"Blessed is the man unto whom the LORD imputeth not iniquity, and in whose spirit there is no guile."—Psalm 32:2.

The highest reward for a man's toil is not what he gets for it, but what he becomes by it.
−John Ruskin

Character is always lost when a high ideal is sacrificed on the altar of conformity and popularity.
−Charles Spurgeon

84

KINDNESS

Kindness is much more than a single act; it is an attitude of the
heart that causes you to be aware of the needs of others.

"And be ye kind one to another, tenderhearted, forgiving
one another, even as God for Christ's sake hath forgiven
you."—Ephesians 4:32.

"Then shall the King say unto them on his right hand,
Come, ye blessed of my Father, inherit the kingdom prepared
for you from the foundation of the world: For I was an
hungred, and ye gave me meat: I was thirsty, and ye gave me
drink: I was a stranger, and ye took me in: Naked, and ye
clothed me: I was sick, and ye visited me: I was in prison,
and ye came unto me."—Matthew 25:34–36.

"Put on therefore, as the elect of God, holy and beloved,
bowels of mercies, kindness, humbleness of mind, meekness,
longsuffering."—Colossians 3:12.

"And if ye lend to them of whom ye hope to receive, what
thank have ye? for sinners also lend to sinners, to receive as
much again. But love ye your enemies, and do good, and
lend, hoping for nothing again; and your reward shall be
great, and ye shall be the children of the Highest: for he is
kind unto the unthankful and to the evil."—Luke 6:34,35.

"And beside this, giving all diligence, add to your faith
virtue; and to virtue knowledge; And to knowledge temperance; and to temperance patience; and to patience godliness;
And to godliness brotherly kindness; and to brotherly kindness charity."—II Peter 1:5–7.

"Because thy lovingkindness is better than life, my lips
shall praise thee."—Psalm 63:3.

"And he said, Blessed be thou of the LORD, my daughter: for thou hast shewed more kindness in the latter end than at the beginning, inasmuch as thou followedst not young men, whether poor or rich." —Ruth 3:10.

"For his merciful kindness is great toward us: and the truth of the LORD endureth for ever. Praise ye the LORD." — Psalm 117:2.

"Let, I pray thee, thy merciful kindness be for my comfort, according to thy word unto thy servant." —Psalm 119:76.

"She openeth her mouth with wisdom; and in her tongue is the law of kindness." —Proverbs 31:26.

"And Naomi said unto her two daughters in law, Go, return each to her mother's house: the LORD deal kindly with you, as ye have dealt with the dead, and with me." —Ruth 1:8.

"Be kindly affectioned one to another with brotherly love; in honour preferring one another." —Romans 12:10.

"In a little wrath I hid my face from thee for a moment; but with everlasting kindness will I have mercy on thee, saith the LORD thy Redeemer." —Isaiah 54:8.

"Go and cry in the ears of Jerusalem, saying, Thus saith the LORD; I remember thee, the kindness of thy youth, the love of thine espousals, when thou wentest after me in the wilderness, in a land that was not sown." —Jeremiah 2:2.

Kindness makes a fellow feel good, whether it's being done to him or by him.
—Frank A. Clark

KNOWLEDGE

What a person knows. The sum of the information a person has poured into his or her mind.

"And beside this, giving all diligence, add to your faith virtue; and to virtue knowledge."—II Peter 1:5.

"Then shalt thou understand the fear of the LORD, and find the knowledge of God. For the LORD giveth wisdom: out of his mouth cometh knowledge and understanding."—Proverbs 2:5,6.

"And the LORD hath given me knowledge of it, and I know it: then thou shewedst me their doings."—Jeremiah 11:18.

"The heart of the prudent getteth knowledge; and the ear of the wise seeketh knowledge."—Proverbs 18:15.

"Children in whom was no blemish, but well favoured, and skilful in all wisdom, and cunning in knowledge, and understanding science, and such as had ability in them to stand in the king's palace, and whom they might teach the learning and the tongue of the Chaldeans."—Daniel 1:4.

"Trust in the LORD with all thine heart; and lean not unto thine own understanding. In all thy ways acknowledge him, and he shall direct thy paths."—Proverbs 3:5,6.

"Who is this that darkeneth counsel by words without knowledge?"—Job 38:2.

"And this I pray, that your love may abound yet more and more in knowledge and in all judgment."—Philippians 1:9.

"For I bear them record that they have a zeal of God, but not according to knowledge."—Romans 10:2.

"That their hearts might be comforted, being knit together in love, and unto all riches of the full assurance of understanding, to the acknowledgement of the mystery of God, and of the Father, and of Christ; In whom are hid all the treasures of wisdom and knowledge."—Colossians 2:2,3.

"A scorner seeketh wisdom, and findeth it not: but knowledge is easy unto him that understandeth."—Proverbs 14:6.

"But grow in grace, and in the knowledge of our Lord and Saviour Jesus Christ. To him be glory both now and for ever. Amen."—II Peter 3:18.

"Therefore as ye abound in every thing, in faith, and utterance, and knowledge, and in all diligence, and in your love to us, see that ye abound in this grace also."—II Corinthians 8:7.

"The eyes of the LORD preserve knowledge, and he overthroweth the words of the transgressor."—Proverbs 22:12.

"A wise man is strong; yea, a man of knowledge increaseth strength."—Proverbs 24:5.

Knowing is not enough; we must apply.
Willing is not enough; we must do.

–Goethe

The trouble with the world is not that people
know too little, but that they know
so many things that ain't so.

–Mark Twain

LEADERSHIP

Always gathering knowledge from those around you, compiling
the information and returning it to the followers. True
leadership ability is a gift from God. It can be
honed, but it is originally from God.

*"Finally, be ye all of one mind, having compassion one
of another, love as brethren, be pitiful, be courteous."*—
I Peter 3:8.

*"For the leaders of this people cause them to err; and they
that are led of them are destroyed."*—Isaiah 9:16.

*"And I will give you pastors according to mine heart,
which shall feed you with knowledge and understanding."*—
Jeremiah 3:15.

*"Let us hear the conclusion of the whole matter: Fear
God, and keep his commandments: for this is the whole duty
of man."*—Ecclesiastes 12:13.

*"Where no counsel is, the people fall: but in the multitude
of counsellors there is safety."*—Proverbs 11:14.

*"And he saith unto them, Follow me, and I will make you
fishers of men. And they straightway left their nets, and
followed him."*—Matthew 4:19,20.

*"Be kindly affectioned one to another with brotherly love;
in honour preferring one another."*—Romans 12:10.

*"The hand of the diligent shall bear rule: but the slothful
shall be under tribute."*—Proverbs 12:24.

GET A GRIP!

"Thou shalt not avenge, nor bear any grudge against the children of thy people, but thou shalt love thy neighbour as thyself: I am the LORD." —Leviticus 19:18.

"If thou forbear to deliver them that are drawn unto death, and those that are ready to be slain; If thou sayest, Behold, we knew it not; doth not he that pondereth the heart consider it? and he that keepeth thy soul, doth not he know it? and shall not he render to every man according to his works?" —Proverbs 24:11, 12.

"Honour all men. Love the brotherhood. Fear God. Honour the king." —I Peter 2:17.

"Ye have heard that it hath been said, Thou shalt love thy neighbour, and hate thine enemy. But I say unto you, Love your enemies, bless them that curse you, do good to them that hate you, and pray for them which despitefully use you, and persecute you." —Matthew 5:43, 44.

"And let us consider one another to provoke unto love and to good works." —Hebrews 10:24.

"And through thy knowledge shall the weak brother perish, for whom Christ died? But when ye sin so against the brethren, and wound their weak conscience, ye sin against Christ." —I Corinthians 8:11, 12.

"Let every one of us please his neighbour for his good to edification." —Romans 15:2.

Leaders think. They think because they are leaders. They are leaders because they think.

—Paul Parker

LOVE OF CHRIST

A love to each individual that is beyond our
most extreme imagination.

"*For God so loved the world, that he gave his only begotten
Son, that whosoever believeth in him should not perish, but
have everlasting life.*"—John 3:16.

"*But that the world may know that I love the Father; and
as the Father gave me commandment, even so I do. Arise, let
us go hence.*"—John 14:31.

"*We love him, because he first loved us.*"—I John 4:19.

"*But God commendeth his love toward us, in that, while
we were yet sinners, Christ died for us.*"—Romans 5:8.

"*The LORD hath appeared of old unto me, saying, Yea, I
have loved thee with an everlasting love: therefore with lovingkindness have I drawn thee.*"—Jeremiah 31:3.

"*For the wages of sin is death; but the gift of God is eternal life through Jesus Christ our Lord.*"—Romans 6:23.

"*For the love of Christ constraineth us; because we
thus judge, that if one died for all, then were all dead.*"—
II Corinthians 5:14.

"*I will heal their backsliding, I will love them freely: for
mine anger is turned away from him.*"—Hosea 14:4.

"*Finally, brethren, farewell. Be perfect, be of good comfort, be of one mind, live in peace; and the God of love and
peace shall be with you.*"—II Corinthians 13:11.

"And to know the love of Christ, which passeth knowledge, that ye might be filled with all the fulness of God."—Ephesians 3:19.

"Beloved, let us love one another: for love is of God; and every one that loveth is born of God, and knoweth God. He that loveth not knoweth not God; for God is love. In this was manifested the love of God toward us, because that God sent his only begotten Son into the world, that we might live through him. Herein is love, not that we loved God, but that he loved us, and sent his Son to be the propitiation for our sins."—I John 4:7-10.

"Love not the world, neither the things that are in the world. If any man love the world, the love of the Father is not in him."—I John 2:15.

"And we have known and believed the love that God hath to us. God is love; and he that dwelleth in love dwelleth in God, and God in him."—I John 4:16.

"Mercy unto you, and peace, and love, be multiplied."—Jude 2.

Most of us want very much to be loved. Perhaps we are not concerned enough about loving.

—Erwin McDonald

MEEKNESS

Not impressed with one's ability or strength. Examples are
Moses and David in the Old Testament.

*"And be ye kind one to another, tenderhearted, forgiving
one another, even as God for Christ's sake hath forgiven
you."*—Ephesians 4:32.

*"The meek shall eat and be satisfied: they shall praise
the LORD that seek him: your heart shall live for ever."*—
Psalm 22:26.

"Blessed are the meek: for they shall inherit the earth."—
Matthew 5:5.

*"For the LORD taketh pleasure in his people: he will beau-
tify the meek with salvation."*—Psalm 149:4.

*"Now the man Moses was very meek, above all the men
which were upon the face of the earth."*—Numbers 12:3.

*"Now I Paul myself beseech you by the meekness and gen-
tleness of Christ, who in presence am base among you, but
being absent am bold toward you."*—II Corinthians 10:1.

*"The discretion of a man deferreth his anger; and it is his
glory to pass over a transgression."*—Proverbs 19:11.

*"Take my yoke upon you, and learn of me; for I am meek
and lowly in heart: and ye shall find rest unto your souls."*—
Matthew 11:29.

*"A soft answer turneth away wrath: but grievous words
stir up anger."*—Proverbs 15:1.

GET A GRIP!

"He that is slow to anger is better than the mighty; and he that ruleth his spirit than he that taketh a city."— Proverbs 16:32.

"Judge not, and ye shall not be judged: condemn not, and ye shall not be condemned: forgive, and ye shall be forgiven."— Luke 6:37.

"Mercy and truth are met together; righteousness and peace have kissed each other. Truth shall spring out of the earth; and righteousness shall look down from heaven."— Psalm 85:10, 11.

"Great peace have they which love thy law: and nothing shall offend them."—Psalm 119:165.

"But the meek shall inherit the earth; and shall delight themselves in the abundance of peace."—Psalm 37:11.

Meekness is power under control.

–Unknown

MONEY

Monetary means to be used to buy the necessities, to
give to the Lord's work and to help others.

"For the love of money is the root of all evil: which while
some coveted after, they have erred from the faith, and pierced
themselves through with many sorrows."—I Timothy 6:10.

"He that loveth silver shall not be satisfied with silver;
nor he that loveth abundance with increase: this is also
vanity."—Ecclesiastes 5:10.

"But my God shall supply all your need according to his
riches in glory by Christ Jesus."—Philippians 4:19.

"Honour the LORD with thy substance, and with the first-
fruits of all thine increase: So shall thy barns be filled with
plenty, and thy presses shall burst out with new wine."—
Proverbs 3:9,10.

"A little that a righteous man hath is better than the riches
of many wicked."—Psalm 37:16.

"No man can serve two masters: for either he will hate the
one, and love the other; or else he will hold to the one, and
despise the other. Ye cannot serve God and mammon."—
Matthew 6:24.

"Charge them that are rich in this world, that they be not
highminded, nor trust in uncertain riches, but in the living
God, who giveth us richly all things to enjoy."—I Timothy 6:17.

"Wealth gotten by vanity shall be diminished: but he that
gathereth by labour shall increase."—Proverbs 13:11.

"Give, and it shall be given unto you; good measure, pressed down, and shaken together, and running over, shall men give into your bosom. For with the same measure that ye mete withal it shall be measured to you again."—Luke 6:38.

"Ho, every one that thirsteth, come ye to the waters, and he that hath no money; come ye, buy, and eat; yea, come, buy wine and milk without money and without price. Wherefore do ye spend money for that which is not bread? and your labour for that which satisfieth not? hearken diligently unto me, and eat ye that which is good, and let your soul delight itself in fatness."—Isaiah 55:1, 2.

"Better is little with the fear of the LORD than great treasure and trouble therewith."—Proverbs 15:16.

"Let your conversation be without covetousness; and be content with such things as ye have: for he hath said, I will never leave thee, nor forsake thee."—Hebrews 13:5.

"Not that I speak in respect of want: for I have learned, in whatsoever state I am, therewith to be content. I know both how to be abased, and I know how to abound: every where and in all things I am instructed both to be full and to be hungry, both to abound and to suffer need."—Philippians 4:11, 12.

If your outgo exceeds your income, then your upkeep will be your downfall.

−Unknown

MUSIC

Music is the universal language of mankind. Beautiful
melodies are gifts from God. He speaks of music
more than five hundred times in His Word.

*"Praise him with the sound of the trumpet: praise him
with the psaltery and harp. Praise him with the timbrel and
dance: praise him with stringed instruments and organs.
Praise him upon the loud cymbals: praise him upon the
high sounding cymbals."*—Psalm 150:3–5.

"Serve the LORD *with gladness: come before his presence
with singing."*—Psalm 100:2.

*"When the morning stars sang together, and all the sons
of God shouted for joy?"*—Job 38:7.

"I will sing of mercy and judgment: unto thee, O LORD,
will I sing."—Psalm 101:1.

*"But I have trusted in thy mercy; my heart shall rejoice in
thy salvation. I will sing unto the* LORD, *because he hath
dealt bountifully with me."*—Psalm 13:5,6.

*"Let the word of Christ dwell in you richly in all wisdom;
teaching and admonishing one another in psalms and
hymns and spiritual songs, singing with grace in your
hearts to the Lord."*—Colossians 3:16.

*"And at midnight Paul and Silas prayed, and sang praises
unto God: and the prisoners heard them."*—Acts 16:25.

"O come, let us sing unto the LORD: *let us make a joyful
noise to the rock of our salvation."*—Psalm 95:1.

"It came even to pass, as the trumpeters and singers were as one, to make one sound to be heard in praising and thanking the LORD; and when they lifted up their voice with the trumpets and cymbals and instruments of musick, and praised the LORD, saying, For he is good; for his mercy endureth for ever: that then the house was filled with a cloud, even the house of the LORD."—II Chronicles 5:13.

"And he hath put a new song in my mouth, even praise unto our God: many shall see it, and fear, and shall trust in the LORD."—Psalm 40:3.

"Sing unto the LORD with thanksgiving; sing praise upon the harp unto our God."—Psalm 147:7.

"The LORD thy God in the midst of thee is mighty; he will save, he will rejoice over thee with joy; he will rest in his love, he will joy over thee with singing."—Zephaniah 3:17.

"O sing unto the LORD a new song: sing unto the LORD, all the earth."—Psalm 96:1.

"The whole earth is at rest, and is quiet: they break forth into singing."—Isaiah 14:7.

"Sing unto him, sing psalms unto him: talk ye of all his wondrous works."—Psalm 105:2.

"Praise ye the LORD: for it is good to sing praises unto our God; for it is pleasant; and praise is comely."—Psalm 147:1.

I learned more about the Bible through music than any other way.

—Mrs. John R. Rice

OBEDIENCE

Every Christian's peace and happiness is wrapped up in
obedience to God. It starts when wee children
begin to be obedient to parents.

"Children, obey your parents in all things: for this is well
pleasing unto the Lord."—Colossians 3:20.

"Obey them that have the rule over you, and submit yourselves: for they watch for your souls, as they that must give
account, that they may do it with joy, and not with grief: for
that is unprofitable for you."—Hebrews 13:17.

"For to this end also did I write, that I might know
the proof of you, whether ye be obedient in all things."—
II Corinthians 2:9.

"By this we know that we love the children of God, when
we love God, and keep his commandments. For this is the
love of God, that we keep his commandments: and his
commandments are not grievous."—I John 5:2,3.

"For not the hearers of the law are just before God, but the
doers of the law shall be justified."—Romans 2:13.

"Let every soul be subject unto the higher powers. For
there is no power but of God: the powers that be are
ordained of God."—Romans 13:1.

"Blessed are they that keep his testimonies, and that seek
him with the whole heart."—Psalm 119:2.

"Then Peter and the other apostles answered and said,
We ought to obey God rather than men."—Acts 5:29.

"Wherefore gird up the loins of your mind, be sober, and hope to the end for the grace that is to be brought unto you at the revelation of Jesus Christ; As obedient children, not fashioning yourselves according to the former lusts in your ignorance."—I Peter 1:13, 14.

"By faith Abraham, when he was called to go out into a place which he should after receive for an inheritance, obeyed; and he went out, not knowing whither he went."—Hebrews 11:8.

"And we are his witnesses of these things; and so is also the Holy Ghost, whom God hath given to them that obey him."—Acts 5:32.

"Ye shall observe to do therefore as the LORD your God hath commanded you: ye shall not turn aside to the right hand or to the left."—Deuteronomy 5:32.

"But Peter and John answered and said unto them, Whether it be right in the sight of God to hearken unto you more than unto God, judge ye. For we cannot but speak the things which we have seen and heard."—Acts 4:19, 20.

The golden rule for understanding spiritually is not intellect, but obedience. If a man wants...insight into what Jesus Christ teaches, he can only get it by obedience.

—Oswald Chambers

OTHERS

Focusing outside yourself. Jesus' second
favorite commandment.

"We then that are strong ought to bear the infirmities of the weak, and not to please ourselves."—Romans 15:1.

"And thou shalt love the Lord thy God with all thy heart, and with all thy soul, and with all thy mind, and with all thy strength: this is the first commandment. And the second is like, namely this, Thou shalt love thy neighbour as thyself. There is none other commandment greater than these."—Mark 12:30,31.

"A friend loveth at all times, and a brother is born for adversity."—Proverbs 17:17.

"But I say unto you which hear, Love your enemies, do good to them which hate you."—Luke 6:27.

"This is my commandment, That ye love one another, as I have loved you."—John 15:12.

"Honour all men. Love the brotherhood. Fear God. Honour the king."—I Peter 2:17.

"He that hath pity upon the poor lendeth unto the LORD; and that which he hath given will he pay him again."—Proverbs 19:17.

"Bear ye one another's burdens, and so fulfil the law of Christ."—Galatians 6:2.

GET A GRIP!

"But a certain Samaritan, as he journeyed, came where he was: and when he saw him, he had compassion on him, And went to him, and bound up his wounds, pouring in oil and wine, and set him on his own beast, and brought him to an inn, and took care of him." —Luke 10:33,34.

"He that hath a bountiful eye shall be blessed; for he giveth of his bread to the poor." —Proverbs 22:9.

"And if thou draw out thy soul to the hungry, and satisfy the afflicted soul; then shall thy light rise in obscurity, and thy darkness be as the noon day." —Isaiah 58:10.

"Therefore all things whatsoever ye would that men should do to you, do ye even so to them: for this is the law and the prophets." —Matthew 7:12.

"A man that hath friends must shew himself friendly: and there is a friend that sticketh closer than a brother." — Proverbs 18:24.

Help me in all the work I do to ever be sincere and true and know that all I'd do for You must needs be done for others.

—C. D. Meigs

PARENTS

Mom and Dad

"Obey them that have the rule over you, and submit your-selves: for they watch for your souls, as they that must give account, that they may do it with joy, and not with grief: for that is unprofitable for you."—Hebrews 13:17.

"Correct thy son, and he shall give thee rest; yea, he shall give delight unto thy soul."—Proverbs 29:17.

"Children, obey your parents in the Lord: for this is right. Honour thy father and mother; which is the first command-ment with promise; That it may be well with thee, and thou mayest live long on the earth."—Ephesians 6:1–3.

"Honour thy father and thy mother: that thy days may be long upon the land which the LORD thy God giveth thee."—Exodus 20:12.

"House and riches are the inheritance of fathers: and a prudent wife is from the LORD."—Proverbs 19:14.

"When my father and my mother forsake me, then the LORD will take me up."—Psalm 27:10.

"The father of the righteous shall greatly rejoice: and he that begetteth a wise child shall have joy of him. Thy father and thy mother shall be glad, and she that bare thee shall rejoice."—Proverbs 23:24,25.

"Whoso robbeth his father or his mother, and saith, It is no transgression; the same is the companion of a destroyer."—Proverbs 28:24.

"Foolishness is bound in the heart of a child; but the rod of correction shall drive it far from him."—Proverbs 22:15.

"For I know him, that he will command his children and his household after him, and they shall keep the way of the LORD, to do justice and judgment; that the LORD may bring upon Abraham that which he hath spoken of him."—Genesis 18:19.

"Ye shall fear every man his mother, and his father, and keep my sabbaths: I am the LORD your God."—Leviticus 19:3.

"Only take heed to thyself, and keep thy soul diligently, lest thou forget the things which thine eyes have seen, and lest they depart from thy heart all the days of thy life: but teach them thy sons, and thy sons' sons."—Deuteronomy 4:9.

"Behold, the third time I am ready to come to you; and I will not be burdensome to you: for I seek not your's, but you: for the children ought not to lay up for the parents, but the parents for the children."—II Corinthians 12:14.

"Whoso curseth his father or his mother, his lamp shall be put out in obscure darkness."—Proverbs 20:20.

Good parents are not afraid to be momentarily disliked by children during the act of enforcing rules.

—Jean Laird

PATIENCE

Accepting the unalterable timing of events and agendas in one's own life. Waiting until the right time to resolve a problem.

"But in all things approving ourselves as the ministers of God, in much patience, in afflictions, in necessities, in distresses." —II Corinthians 6:4.

"But that on the good ground are they, which in an honest and good heart, having heard the word, keep it, and bring forth fruit with patience." —Luke 8:15.

"Rejoicing in hope; patient in tribulation; continuing instant in prayer." —Romans 12:12.

"But if we hope for that we see not, then do we with patience wait for it." —Romans 8:25.

"And not only so, but we glory in tribulations also: knowing that tribulation worketh patience." —Romans 5:3.

"Be patient therefore, brethren, unto the coming of the Lord. Behold, the husbandman waiteth for the precious fruit of the earth, and hath long patience for it, until he receive the early and latter rain. Be ye also patient; stablish your hearts: for the coming of the Lord draweth nigh." — James 5:7,8.

"For whatsoever things were written aforetime were written for our learning, that we through patience and comfort of the scriptures might have hope. Now the God of patience and consolation grant you to be likeminded one toward another according to Christ Jesus." —Romans 15:4,5.

"Strengthened with all might, according to his glorious power, unto all patience and longsuffering with joyfulness."—Colossians 1:11.

"So that we ourselves glory in you in the churches of God for your patience and faith in all your persecutions and tribulations that ye endure."—II Thessalonians 1:4.

"But thou, O man of God, flee these things; and follow after righteousness, godliness, faith, love, patience, meekness."—I Timothy 6:11.

"That the aged men be sober, grave, temperate, sound in faith, in charity, in patience."—Titus 2:2.

"For ye have need of patience, that, after ye have done the will of God, ye might receive the promise."—Hebrews 10:36.

"Wherefore seeing we also are compassed about with so great a cloud of witnesses, let us lay aside every weight, and the sin which doth so easily beset us, and let us run with patience the race that is set before us."—Hebrews 12:1.

"Knowing this, that the trying of your faith worketh patience. But let patience have her perfect work, that ye may be perfect and entire, wanting nothing."—James 1:3,4.

"And beside this, giving all diligence, add to your faith virtue; and to virtue knowledge; And to knowledge temperance; and to temperance patience; and to patience godliness."—II Peter 1:5,6.

Like farmers, we must realize that we can't sow and reap the same day.

–Unknown

PEER PRESSURE

An attitude of succumbing to the influence of others is one of
the most dangerous dispositions a teen can possess.

*"Wherefore come out from among them, and be ye sepa-
rate, saith the Lord, and touch not the unclean thing; and I
will receive you, And will be a Father unto you, and ye shall
be my sons and daughters, saith the Lord Almighty. Having
therefore these promises, dearly beloved, let us cleanse ourselves from all filthiness of the flesh and spirit, perfecting
holiness in the fear of God."*—II Corinthians 6:17–7:1.

*"As obedient children, not fashioning yourselves according
to the former lusts in your ignorance: But as he which
hath called you is holy, so be ye holy in all manner of conversation; Because it is written, Be ye holy; for I am holy."*—
I Peter 1:14–16.

"Abstain from all appearance of evil."—I Thessalonians
5:22.

*"But put ye on the Lord Jesus Christ, and make not
provision for the flesh, to fulfill the lusts thereof."*—
Romans 13:14.

*"And ye know that he was manifested to take away our
sins; and in him is no sin. Whosoever abideth in him sinneth
not: whosoever sinneth hath not seen him, neither known
him."*—I John 3:5, 6.

*"I will meditate in thy precepts, and have respect unto thy
ways. I will delight myself in thy statutes: I will not forget
thy word."*—Psalm 119:15, 16.

"And now, little children, abide in him; that, when he shall appear, we may have confidence, and not be ashamed before him at his coming."—I John 2:28.

"I beseech you therefore, brethren, by the mercies of God, that ye present your bodies a living sacrifice, holy, acceptable unto God, which is your reasonable service. And be not conformed to this world: but be ye transformed by the renewing of your mind, that ye may prove what is that good, and acceptable, and perfect, will of God."—Romans 12:1,2.

"Depart from evil, and do good; seek peace, and pursue it."—Psalm 34:14.

"Let no man despise thy youth; but be thou an example of the believers, in word, in conversation, in charity, in spirit, in faith, in purity."—I Timothy 4:12.

Some people would have higher principles if it weren't for their interests.

–Lucille S. Harper

You damage yourself and your relations with other people if you think either too much or too little of yourself.

–Marion Jacobson

PRAYER

The greatest power and privilege at our disposal—
communication with our Heavenly Father.

"And this is the confidence that we have in him, that,
if we ask any thing according to his will, he heareth us:
And if we know that he hear us, whatsoever we ask, we
know that we have the petitions that we desired of him."—
I John 5:14, 15.

"Is any among you afflicted? let him pray. Is any merry?
let him sing psalms....Confess your faults one to another,
and pray one for another, that ye may be healed. The
effectual fervent prayer of a righteous man availeth much.
Elias was a man subject to like passions as we are, and he
prayed earnestly that it might not rain: and it rained not on
the earth by the space of three years and six months."—
James 5:13, 16, 17.

"Praying always with all prayer and supplication in the
Spirit, and watching thereunto with all perseverance and
supplication for all saints."—Ephesians 6:18.

"If ye abide in me, and my words abide in you, ye shall
ask what ye will, and it shall be done unto you."—John 15:7.

"And I say unto you, Ask, and it shall be given you; seek,
and ye shall find; knock, and it shall be opened unto you."—
Luke 11:9.

"And whatsoever we ask, we receive of him, because we
keep his commandments, and do those things that are pleasing in his sight."—I John 3:22.

"Again I say unto you, That if two of you shall agree on earth as touching any thing that they shall ask, it shall be done for them of my Father which is in heaven."—Matthew 18:19.

"Therefore I say unto you, What things soever ye desire, when ye pray, believe that ye receive them, and ye shall have them."—Mark 11:24.

"But I say unto you, Love your enemies, bless them that curse you, do good to them that hate you, and pray for them which despitefully use you, and persecute you."—Matthew 5:44.

"The sacrifice of the wicked is an abomination to the LORD: but the prayer of the upright is his delight."—Proverbs 15:8.

"What is it then? I will pray with the spirit, and I will pray with the understanding also: I will sing with the spirit, and I will sing with the understanding also."—I Corinthians 14:15.

"Rejoicing in hope; patient in tribulation; continuing instant in prayer."—Romans 12:12.

It is strange that in our praying we seldom ask for a change of character, but a change in circumstances.

—Unknown

110

PRIORITIES

Keeping first things first, and the main things main.

"*But seek ye first the kingdom of God, and his righteous-ness; and all these things shall be added unto you.*"—Matthew 6:33.

"*He that goeth forth and weepeth, bearing precious seed, shall doubtless come again with rejoicing, bringing his sheaves with him.*"—Psalm 126:6.

"*Study to shew thyself approved unto God, a workman that needeth not to be ashamed, rightly dividing the word of truth.*"—II Timothy 2:15.

"*And Jesus answered him, The first of all the command-ments is, Hear, O Israel; The Lord our God is one Lord: And thou shalt love the Lord thy God with all thy heart, and with all thy soul, and with all thy mind, and with all thy strength: this is the first commandment.*"—Mark 12:29,30.

"*Wherewithal shall a young man cleanse his way? by taking heed thereto according to thy word.*"—Psalm 119:9.

"*My son, forget not my law; but let thine heart keep my commandments: For length of days, and long life, and peace, shall they add to thee.*"—Proverbs 3:1,2.

"*Wherefore glorify ye the LORD in the fires, even the name of the LORD God of Israel in the isles of the sea.*"—Isaiah 24:15.

"*Wherefore, if God so clothe the grass of the field, which to day is, and to morrow is cast into the oven, shall he not much more clothe you, O ye of little faith?*"—Matthew 6:30.

GET A GRIP!

"Thy word have I hid in mine heart, that I might not sin against thee."—Psalm 119:11.

"Honour the LORD with thy substance, and with the first-fruits of all thine increase: So shall thy barns be filled with plenty, and thy presses shall burst out with new wine."—Proverbs 3:9,10.

"It is a good thing to give thanks unto the LORD, and to sing praises unto thy name, O most High."—Psalm 92:1.

"Let no man despise thy youth; but be thou an example of the believers, in word, in conversation, in charity, in spirit, in faith, in purity."—I Timothy 4:12.

"Let your light so shine before men, that they may see your good works, and glorify your Father which is in heaven."—Matthew 5:16.

"Labour not to be rich: cease from thine own wisdom."—Proverbs 23:4.

"So teach us to number our days, that we may apply our hearts unto wisdom."—Psalm 90:12.

The older I get, the more wisdom I find in the ancient rule of taking first things first—a process which often reduces the most complex human problem to manageable proportion.
—Dwight Eisenhower

The last thing one knows is what to put first.
—Blaise Pascal

PROBLEMS

Opportunities for learning experiences;
sometimes small, and other times great.

"*Trust in the LORD with all thine heart; and lean not unto thine own understanding. In all thy ways acknowledge him, and he shall direct thy paths.*"—Proverbs 3:5, 6.

"*He shall call upon me, and I will answer him: I will be with him in trouble; I will deliver him, and honour him.*"—Psalm 91:15.

"*But we have this treasure in earthen vessels, that the excellency of the power may be of God, and not of us. We are troubled on every side, yet not distressed; we are perplexed, but not in despair.*"—II Corinthians 4:7, 8.

"*Be not far from me; for trouble is near; for there is none to help.*"—Psalm 22:11.

"*Let your conversation be without covetousness; and be content with such things as ye have: for he hath said, I will never leave thee, nor forsake thee. So that we may boldly say, The Lord is my helper, and I will not fear what man shall do unto me.*"—Hebrews 13:5, 6.

"*Nay, in all these things we are more than conquerors through him that loved us.*"—Romans 8:37.

"*He healeth the broken in heart, and bindeth up their wounds.*"—Psalm 147:3.

"*I can do all things through Christ which strengtheneth me.*"—Philippians 4:13.

GET A GRIP!

"Take my yoke upon you, and learn of me; for I am meek and lowly in heart: and ye shall find rest unto your souls. For my yoke is easy, and my burden is light."—Matthew 11:29,30.

"Which hope we have as an anchor of the soul, both sure and stedfast, and which entereth into that within the veil."—Hebrews 6:19.

"He giveth power to the faint; and to them that have no might he increaseth strength."—Isaiah 40:29.

"Many are the afflictions of the righteous: but the LORD delivereth him out of them all."—Psalm 34:19.

"Finally, brethren, whatsoever things are true, whatsoever things are honest, whatsoever things are just, whatsoever things are pure, whatsoever things are lovely, whatsoever things are of good report; if there be any virtue, and if there be any praise, think on these things."—Philippians 4:8.

"Whoso keepeth his mouth and his tongue keepeth his soul from troubles."—Proverbs 21:23.

"I sought the LORD, and he heard me, and delivered me from all my fears. They looked unto him, and were lightened: and their faces were not ashamed. This poor man cried, and the LORD heard him, and saved him out of all his troubles."—Psalm 34:4–6.

Most people spend more time and energy going around problems than in trying to solve them.

–Henry Ford

PROCRASTINATION

Delaying the carrying out of important tasks
until it is past the best time of action.

"Go to the ant, thou sluggard; consider her ways, and be
wise: Which having no guide, overseer, or ruler, Provideth
her meat in the summer, and gathereth her food in the harvest."—Proverbs 6:6–8.

"Walk in wisdom toward them that are without, redeeming
the time."—Colossians 4:5.

"The soul of the sluggard desireth, and hath nothing: but
the soul of the diligent shall be made fat."—Proverbs 13:4.

"And they said, Arise, that we may go up against them:
for we have seen the land, and, behold, it is very good: and
are ye still? be not slothful to go, and to enter to possess the
land."—Judges 18:9.

"I went by the field of the slothful, and by the vineyard of
the man void of understanding."—Proverbs 24:30.

"The sluggard will not plow by reason of the cold;
therefore shall he beg in harvest, and have nothing."—
Proverbs 20:4.

"This book of the law shall not depart out of thy mouth;
but thou shalt meditate therein day and night, that thou
mayest observe to do according to all that is written therein:
for then thou shalt make thy way prosperous, and then thou
shalt have good success."—Joshua 1:8.

"The hand of the diligent shall bear rule: but the slothful
shall be under tribute."—Proverbs 12:24.

"I must work the works of him that sent me, while it is day: the night cometh, when no man can work." —John 9:4.

"He also that is slothful in his work is brother to him that is a great waster." —Proverbs 18:9.

"Let us hold fast the profession of our faith without wavering; (for he is faithful that promised;)" —Hebrews 10:23.

"A prudent man foreseeth the evil, and hideth himself: but the simple pass on, and are punished." —Proverbs 22:3.

"For we are made partakers of Christ, if we hold the beginning of our confidence stedfast unto the end." —Hebrews 3:14.

Procrastination is not only the thief of time; it is also the grave of opportunity.

—Unknown

PROMISES OF GOD

The only promises that you can count on—
every time, any time, all the time.

"For all the promises of God in him are yea, and in him Amen, unto the glory of God by us."—II Corinthians 1:20.

"Trust in the LORD with all thine heart; and lean not unto thine own understanding. In all thy ways acknowledge him, and he shall direct thy paths."—Proverbs 3:5, 6.

"Call unto me, and I will answer thee, and shew thee great and mighty things, which thou knowest not."—Jeremiah 33:3.

"Let us hold fast the profession of our faith without wavering; (for he is faithful that promised;)"—Hebrews 10:23.

"Blessed is the man that walketh not in the counsel of the ungodly, nor standeth in the way of sinners, nor sitteth in the seat of the scornful. But his delight is in the law of the LORD; and in his law doth he meditate day and night. And he shall be like a tree planted by the rivers of water, that bringeth forth his fruit in his season; his leaf also shall not wither; and whatsoever he doeth shall prosper."—Psalm 1:1–3.

"For God so loved the world, that he gave his only begotten Son, that whosoever believeth in him should not perish, but have everlasting life."—John 3:16.

"He staggered not at the promise of God through unbelief; but was strong in faith, giving glory to God; And being fully persuaded that, what he had promised, he was able also to perform."—Romans 4:20, 21.

117

"That ye be not slothful, but followers of them who through faith and patience inherit the promises."—Hebrews 6:12.

"Whereby are given unto us exceeding great and precious promises: that by these ye might be partakers of the divine nature, having escaped the corruption that is in the world through lust."—II Peter 1:4.

"The Lord is not slack concerning his promise, as some men count slackness; but is longsuffering to us-ward, not willing that any should perish, but that all should come to repentance."—II Peter 3:9.

"Through faith also Sara herself received strength to conceive seed, and was delivered of a child when she was past age, because she judged him faithful who had promised."—Hebrews 11:11.

"And this is the promise that he hath promised us, even eternal life."—I John 2:25.

"Who are Israelites; to whom pertaineth the adoption, and the glory, and the covenants, and the giving of the law, and the service of God, and the promises."—Romans 9:4.

**God never made a promise that
was too good to be true.**

–Dwight L. Moody

PUNISHMENT

A penalty imposed for wrongdoing. Christ
took our punishment for us.

"For Christ also hath once suffered for sins, the just for
the unjust, that he might bring us to God, being put to death
in the flesh, but quickened by the Spirit."—I Peter 3:18.

"The wicked shall be turned into hell, and all the nations
that forget God."—Psalm 9:17.

"For they have sown the wind, and they shall reap the
whirlwind: it hath no stalk: the bud shall yield no meal: if
so be it yield, the strangers shall swallow it up."—Hosea 8:7.

"Sow to yourselves in righteousness, reap in mercy; break
up your fallow ground: for it is time to seek the LORD, till he
come and rain righteousness upon you."—Hosea 10:12.

"All we like sheep have gone astray; we have turned every
one to his own way; and the LORD hath laid on him the
iniquity of us all."—Isaiah 53:6.

"And, having made peace through the blood of his cross,
by him to reconcile all things unto himself; by him, I say,
whether they be things in earth, or things in heaven. And
you, that were sometime alienated and enemies in your
mind by wicked works, yet now hath he reconciled."—
Colossians 1:20,21.

"For God so loved the world, that he gave his only begotten
Son, that whosoever believeth in him should not perish, but
have everlasting life."—John 3:16.

"He that covereth his sins shall not prosper: but whoso confesseth and forsaketh them shall have mercy."—Proverbs 28:13.

"But if the wicked will turn from all his sins that he hath committed, and keep all my statutes, and do that which is lawful and right, he shall surely live, he shall not die."—Ezekiel 18:21.

"Blotting out the handwriting of ordinances that was against us, which was contrary to us, and took it out of the way, nailing it to his cross."—Colossians 2:14.

"But God commendeth his love toward us, in that, while we were yet sinners, Christ died for us."—Romans 5:8.

"Let the wicked forsake his way, and the unrighteous man his thoughts: and let him return unto the LORD, and he will have mercy upon him; and to our God, for he will abundantly pardon."—Isaiah 55:7.

"For the wages of sin is death; but the gift of God is eternal life through Jesus Christ our Lord."—Romans 6:23.

"Be not deceived; God is not mocked: for whatsoever a man soweth, that shall he also reap."—Galatians 6:7.

There are two great injustices that can befall a child. One is to punish him for something he didn't do. The other is to let him get away with doing something he knows is wrong.

–Robert Gardner

PURITY

Living in a Biblical manner that allows a
good conscience at the end of the day.

"Finally, brethren, whatsoever things are true, whatsoever things are honest, whatsoever things are just, whatsoever things are pure, whatsoever things are lovely, whatsoever things are of good report; if there be any virtue, and if there be any praise, think on these things."—Philippians 4:8.

"He that loveth pureness of heart, for the grace of his lips the king shall be his friend."—Proverbs 22:11.

"If thou wert pure and upright; surely now he would awake for thee, and make the habitation of thy righteousness prosperous."—Job 8:6.

"Even a child is known by his doings, whether his work be pure, and whether it be right."—Proverbs 20:11.

"Lay hands suddenly on no man, neither be partaker of other men's sins: keep thyself pure."—I Timothy 5:22.

"The thoughts of the wicked are an abomination to the LORD: but the words of the pure are pleasant words."—Proverbs 15:26.

"Unto the pure all things are pure: but unto them that are defiled and unbelieving is nothing pure; but even their mind and conscience is defiled."—Titus 1:15.

"But the wisdom that is from above is first pure, then peaceable, gentle, and easy to be intreated, full of mercy and good fruits, without partiality, and without hypocrisy."—James 3:17.

"This second epistle, beloved, I now write unto you; in both which I stir up your pure minds by way of remembrance."—II Peter 3:1.

"And every man that hath this hope in him purifieth himself, even as he is pure."—I John 3:3.

"Who can say, I have made my heart clean, I am pure from my sin?"—Proverbs 20:9.

"The way of man is froward and strange: but as for the pure, his work is right."—Proverbs 21:8.

"By pureness, by knowledge, by longsuffering, by kindness, by the Holy Ghost, by love unfeigned."—II Corinthians 6:6.

Purity is not imposed upon us as though it were a kind of punishment.

—Georges Bernanos

REBELLION

In our kind of day, rebellion has become rampant, even though
man has been guilty of it for centuries. Deliberate disregard
for the rules and regulations that govern our
actions comes at a high cost.

*"For rebellion is as the sin of witchcraft, and stubborn-
ness is as iniquity and idolatry."* —I Samuel 15:23.

*"For I know thy rebellion, and thy stiff neck: behold,
while I am yet alive with you this day, ye have been rebellious against the LORD; and how much more after my
death?"* —Deuteronomy 31:27.

*"The LORD God of gods, the LORD God of gods, he
knoweth, and Israel he shall know; if it be in rebellion, or if
in transgression against the LORD, (save us not this day,)"* —
Joshua 22:22.

*"And might not be as their fathers, a stubborn and rebel-
lious generation; a generation that set not their heart aright,
and whose spirit was not stedfast with God."* —Psalm 78:8.

*"For he addeth rebellion unto his sin, he clappeth his
hands among us, and multiplieth his words against God."* —
Job 34:37.

*"An evil man seeketh only rebellion: therefore a cruel
messenger shall be sent against him."* —Proverbs 17:11.

*"Therefore thus saith the LORD; Behold, I will cast thee
from off the face of the earth: this year thou shalt die,
because thou hast taught rebellion against the LORD."* —
Jeremiah 28:16.

"Therefore thus saith the LORD; Behold, I will punish Shemaiah the Nehelamite, and his seed: he shall not have a man to dwell among this people; neither shall he behold the good that I will do for my people, saith the LORD; because he hath taught rebellion against the LORD."—Jeremiah 29:32.

"If a man have a stubborn and rebellious son, which will not obey the voice of his father, or the voice of his mother, and that, when they have chastened him, will not hearken unto them: Then shall his father and his mother lay hold on him, and bring him out unto the elders of his city, and unto the gate of his place."—Deuteronomy 21:18,19.

"Woe to the rebellious children, saith the LORD, that take counsel, but not of me; and that cover with a covering, but not of my spirit, that they may add sin to sin."—Isaiah 30:1.

"As an adamant harder than flint have I made thy forehead: fear them not, neither be dismayed at their looks, though they be a rebellious house."—Ezekiel 3:9.

"He ruleth by his power for ever; his eyes behold the nations: let not the rebellious exalt themselves. Selah."—Psalm 66:7.

"Children, obey your parents in the Lord: for this is right."—Ephesians 6:1.

No man doth safely rule but he that hath learned gladly to obey.
—Thomas à Kempis

RESPECT

Recognizing the rights, privileges
and positions of others.

"Let your speech be alway with grace, seasoned with salt, that ye may know how ye ought to answer every man."—Colossians 4:6.

"Honour all men. Love the brotherhood. Fear God. Honour the king. Servants, be subject to your masters with all fear; not only to the good and gentle, but also to the froward."—I Peter 2:17,18.

"My glory was fresh in me, and my bow was renewed in my hand. Unto me men gave ear, and waited, and kept silence at my counsel."—Job 29:20,21.

"Rebuke not an elder, but intreat him as a father; and the younger men as brethren; The elder women as mothers; the younger as sisters, with all purity."—I Timothy 5:1,2.

"Hearken unto thy father that begat thee, and despise not thy mother when she is old."—Proverbs 23:22.

"Give her of the fruit of her hands; and let her own works praise her in the gates."—Proverbs 31:31.

"And why call ye me, Lord, Lord, and do not the things which I say?"—Luke 6:46.

"Let the elders that rule well be counted worthy of double honour, especially they who labour in the word and doctrine."—I Timothy 5:17.

"A son honoureth his father, and a servant his master: if then I be a father, where is mine honour? and if I be a master, where is my fear? saith the LORD of hosts unto you, O priests, that despise my name. And ye say, Wherein have we despised thy name?"—Malachi 1:6.

"Likewise, ye younger, submit yourselves unto the elder. Yea, all of you be subject one to another, and be clothed with humility: for God resisteth the proud, and giveth grace to the humble."—I Peter 5:5.

"Blessed is he that readeth, and they that hear the words of this prophecy, and keep those things which are written therein: for the time is at hand."—Revelation 1:3.

"And whosoever shall exalt himself shall be abased; and he that shall humble himself shall be exalted."—Matthew 23:12.

A man who does not respect his own life and that of others robs himself of his dignity as a human being.

–Dalip Singh

RESPONSIBILITY

The ability to be trusted with important tasks, as
well as standing good for acts committed.

"For every man shall bear his own burden."—Galatians 6:5.

*"Even a child is known by his doings, whether his work
be pure, and whether it be right."*—Proverbs 20:11.

*"For unto every one that hath shall be given, and he shall
have abundance: but from him that hath not shall be taken
away even that which he hath."*—Matthew 25:29.

*"How God anointed Jesus of Nazareth with the Holy
Ghost and with power: who went about doing good, and
healing all that were oppressed of the devil; for God was
with him."*—Acts 10:38.

*"Thou madest him to have dominion over the works of thy
hands; thou hast put all things under his feet."*—Psalm 8:6.

"But ye, brethren, be not weary in well doing."—II
Thessalonians 3:13.

*"For by thy words thou shalt be justified, and by thy
words thou shalt be condemned."*—Matthew 12:37.

*"For it is better, if the will of God be so, that ye suffer for
well doing, than for evil doing."*—I Peter 3:17.

*"Wherefore, as by one man sin entered into the world, and
death by sin; and so death passed upon all men, for that all
have sinned."*—Romans 5:12.

"So likewise ye, when ye shall have done all those things which are commanded you, say, We are unprofitable servants: we have done that which was our duty to do."—Luke 17:10.

"We then that are strong ought to bear the infirmities of the weak, and not to please ourselves."—Romans 15:1.

"And let our's also learn to maintain good works for necessary uses, that they be not unfruitful."—Titus 3:14.

"Wherein they think it strange that ye run not with them to the same excess of riot, speaking evil of you: Who shall give account to him that is ready to judge the quick and the dead. For for this cause was the gospel preached also to them that are dead, that they might be judged according to men in the flesh, but live according to God in the spirit."—I Peter 4:4–6.

**You cannot escape the responsibility
of tomorrow by evading it today.**
—Abraham Lincoln

**Some people grow under responsibility.
Others merely swell.**

RIGHTEOUSNESS

Godliness. Living according to Biblical instruction and standards.

"And Jesus answering said unto him, Suffer it to be so now: for thus it becometh us to fulfil all righteousness. Then he suffered him."—Matthew 3:15.

"Offer the sacrifices of righteousness, and put your trust in the LORD."—Psalm 4:5.

"The righteousness of the upright shall deliver them: but transgressors shall be taken in their own naughtiness."—Proverbs 11:6.

"But of him are ye in Christ Jesus, who of God is made unto us wisdom, and righteousness, and sanctification, and redemption."—I Corinthians 1:30.

"He that walketh uprightly, and worketh righteousness, and speaketh the truth in his heart."—Psalm 15:2.

"Blessed are they which do hunger and thirst after righteousness: for they shall be filled."—Matthew 5:6.

"As righteousness tendeth to life: so he that pursueth evil pursueth it to his own death."—Proverbs 11:19.

"He shall receive the blessing from the LORD, and righteousness from the God of his salvation."—Psalm 24:5.

"For with the heart man believeth unto righteousness; and with the mouth confession is made unto salvation."—Romans 10:10.

"Riches profit not in the day of wrath: but righteousness delivereth from death."—Proverbs 11:4.

"In the way of righteousness is life; and in the pathway thereof there is no death."—Proverbs 12:28.

"Better is a little with righteousness than great revenues without right."—Proverbs 16:8.

"Righteousness exalteth a nation: but sin is a reproach to any people."—Proverbs 14:34.

You can't get holy in a hurry, but you can start taking steps in that direction right away.
—Malcolm Cronk

A passion for personal holiness will make you a lot easier to get along with.
—Robert A. Cook

SALVATION

Passing from spiritual death unto everlasting life in Christ.

"Let all those that seek thee rejoice and be glad in thee: and let such as love thy salvation say continually, Let God be magnified."—Psalm 70:4.

"That if thou shalt confess with thy mouth the Lord Jesus, and shalt believe in thine heart that God hath raised him from the dead, thou shalt be saved. For with the heart man believeth unto righteousness; and with the mouth confession is made unto salvation."—Romans 10:9,10.

"Behold, God is my salvation; I will trust, and not be afraid: for the LORD JEHOVAH is my strength and my song; he also is become my salvation."—Isaiah 12:2.

"How shall we escape, if we neglect so great salvation; which at the first began to be spoken by the Lord, and was confirmed unto us by them that heard him."—Hebrews 2:3.

"For whosoever shall call upon the name of the Lord shall be saved."—Romans 10:13.

"So Christ was once offered to bear the sins of many; and unto them that look for him shall he appear the second time without sin unto salvation."—Hebrews 9:28.

"I have longed for thy salvation, O LORD; and thy law is my delight."—Psalm 119:174.

"Neither is there salvation in any other: for there is none other name under heaven given among men, whereby we must be saved."—Acts 4:12.

"For the LORD taketh pleasure in his people: he will beautify the meek with salvation."—Psalm 149:4.

"For I am not ashamed of the gospel of Christ: for it is the power of God unto salvation to every one that believeth; to the Jew first, and also to the Greek."—Romans 1:16.

"For godly sorrow worketh repentance to salvation not to be repented of: but the sorrow of the world worketh death."— II Corinthians 7:10.

"But we are bound to give thanks alway to God for you, brethren beloved of the Lord, because God hath from the beginning chosen you to salvation through sanctification of the Spirit and belief of the truth."—II Thessalonians 2:13.

"I will greatly rejoice in the LORD, my soul shall be joyful in my God; for he hath clothed me with the garments of salvation, he hath covered me with the robe of righteousness, as a bridegroom decketh himself with ornaments, and as a bride adorneth herself with her jewels."—Isaiah 61:10.

"Who are kept by the power of God through faith unto salvation ready to be revealed in the last time."—I Peter 1:5.

God doesn't just patch–He renews.
God doesn't just salve sins–He saves.
God doesn't just reform–He transforms
by His power.
–Merrill C. Tenney

SECURITY OF A BELIEVER

A wonderful assurance that one belongs to the Heavenly
Father forever. Once a person becomes a child of God,
he belongs to God from that moment on.

*"Therefore if any man be in Christ, he is a new creature:
old things are passed away; behold, all things are become
new."*—II Corinthians 5:17.

*"If we confess our sins, he is faithful and just to forgive us
our sins, and to cleanse us from all unrighteousness."*—
I John 1:9.

*"I am the good shepherd, and know my sheep, and am
known of mine."*—John 10:14.

*"By this shall all men know that ye are my disciples, if ye
have love one to another."*—John 13:35.

*"These things have I written unto you that believe on the
name of the Son of God; that ye may know that ye have eternal life, and that ye may believe on the name of the Son of
God."*—I John 5:13.

*"For the which cause I also suffer these things: neverthe-
less I am not ashamed: for I know whom I have believed,
and am persuaded that he is able to keep that which I have
committed unto him against that day."*—II Timothy 1:12.

*"Beloved, now are we the sons of God, and it doth not yet
appear what we shall be: but we know that, when he shall
appear, we shall be like him; for we shall see him as he is."*—
I John 3:2.

"But as many as received him, to them gave he power to become the sons of God, even to them that believe on his name."—John 1:12.

"Whosoever is born of God doth not commit sin; for his seed remaineth in him: and he cannot sin, because he is born of God."—I John 3:9.

"He that believeth on the Son hath everlasting life: and he that believeth not the Son shall not see life; but the wrath of God abideth on him."—John 3:36.

"And they said, Believe on the Lord Jesus Christ, and thou shalt be saved, and thy house."—Acts 16:31.

"The Spirit itself beareth witness with our spirit, that we are the children of God."—Romans 8:16.

"This is he that came by water and blood, even Jesus Christ; not by water only, but by water and blood. And it is the Spirit that beareth witness, because the Spirit is truth."—I John 5:6.

"Who his own self bare our sins in his own body on the tree, that we, being dead to sins, should live unto righteousness: by whose stripes ye were healed."—I Peter 2:24.

**When I am born again from above, I receive
from the Risen Lord His very life....
He completed everything for my
salvation and sanctification.**

–Oswald Chambers

SELF-CONTROL

This characteristic is greatly valued in teens, but is only
made possible through the power of the Holy Spirit
in one's life, and the knowledge of the Bible.

*"Humble yourselves therefore under the mighty hand of
God, that he may exalt you in due time: Casting all your
care upon him; for he careth for you."* —I Peter 5:6,7.

*"But Daniel purposed in his heart that he would not
defile himself with the portion of the king's meat, nor with
the wine which he drank: therefore he requested of the
prince of the eunuchs that he might not defile himself."* —
Daniel 1:8.

*"Let your moderation be known unto all men. The Lord is
at hand."* —Philippians 4:5.

*"For if ye live after the flesh, ye shall die: but if ye through
the Spirit do mortify the deeds of the body, ye shall live."* —
Romans 8:13.

*"Blessed is the man that endureth temptation: for when
he is tried, he shall receive the crown of life, which the Lord
hath promised to them that love him."* —James 1:12.

*"Who are kept by the power of God through faith unto sal-
vation ready to be revealed in the last time."* —I Peter 1:5.

*"And if a man also strive for masteries, yet is he not
crowned, except he strive lawfully."* —II Timothy 2:5.

*"But put ye on the Lord Jesus Christ, and make not pro-
vision for the flesh, to fulfil the lusts thereof."* —Romans 13:14.

GET A GRIP!

"Set a watch, O LORD, before my mouth; keep the door of my lips."—Psalm 141:3.

"Charity suffereth long, and is kind....Doth not behave itself unseemly, seeketh not her own, is not easily provoked, thinketh no evil."—I Corinthians 13:4, 5.

"And to knowledge temperance; and to temperance patience; and to patience godliness."—II Peter 1:6.

"If any man among you seem to be religious, and bridleth not his tongue, but deceiveth his own heart, this man's religion is vain."—James 1:26.

"Know ye not that they which run in a race run all, but one receiveth the prize? So run, that ye may obtain. And every man that striveth for the mastery is temperate in all things. Now they do it to obtain a corruptible crown; but we an incorruptible."—I Corinthians 9:24, 25.

**Self-control involves first knowing
God's guidelines for right living
as found in the Bible.**

—Shawn Harrison

SIN

A transgression of God's law as expressed in the Bible.

"Moreover the law entered, that the offence might abound. But where sin abounded, grace did much more abound."—Romans 5:20.

"Fools make a mock at sin: but among the righteous there is favour."—Proverbs 14:9.

"Righteousness exalteth a nation: but sin is a reproach to any people."—Proverbs 14:34.

"Keep back thy servant also from presumptuous sins; let them not have dominion over me: then shall I be upright, and I shall be innocent from the great transgression."—Psalm 19:13.

"Therefore will I divide him a portion with the great, and he shall divide the spoil with the strong; because he hath poured out his soul unto death: and he was numbered with the transgressors; and he bare the sin of many, and made intercession for the transgressors."—Isaiah 53:12.

"Blessed is he whose transgression is forgiven, whose sin is covered."—Psalm 32:1.

"Wherefore I say unto you, All manner of sin and blasphemy shall be forgiven unto men: but the blasphemy against the Holy Ghost shall not be forgiven unto men."—Matthew 12:31.

"For I will declare mine iniquity; I will be sorry for my sin."—Psalm 38:18.

GET A GRIP!

"The next day John seeth Jesus coming unto him, and saith, Behold the Lamb of God, which taketh away the sin of the world."—John 1:29.

"For I acknowledge my transgressions: and my sin is ever before me."—Psalm 51:3.

"And when he is come, he will reprove the world of sin, and of righteousness, and of judgment."—John 16:8.

"Thou hast set our iniquities before thee, our secret sins in the light of thy countenance."—Psalm 90:8.

"Whatsoever is not of faith is sin."—Romans 14:23.

"For he hath made him to be sin for us, who knew no sin; that we might be made the righteousness of God in him."—II Corinthians 5:21.

"He hath not dealt with us after our sins; nor rewarded us according to our iniquities."—Psalm 103:10.

"Who his own self bare our sins in his own body on the tree, that we, being dead to sins, should live unto righteousness: by whose stripes ye were healed."—I Peter 2:24.

We are too Christian to really enjoy sinning, and too fond of sinning to really enjoy Christianity. Most of us know perfectly well what we ought to do; our trouble is that we do not want to do it.

–Peter Marshall

SPEECH

Your speech allows you to be evaluated and
judged by all who hear you.

"For he that will love life, and see good days, let him
refrain his tongue from evil, and his lips that they speak no
guile."—I Peter 3:10.

"But now ye also put off all these; anger, wrath, malice,
blasphemy, filthy communication out of your mouth."—
Colossians 3:8.

"The tongue of the just is as choice silver: the heart of the
wicked is little worth."—Proverbs 10:20.

"The wicked is snared by the transgression of his lips: but
the just shall come out of trouble."—Proverbs 12:13.

"The mouth of the just bringeth forth wisdom: but the
froward tongue shall be cut out. The lips of the righteous
know what is acceptable: but the mouth of the wicked
speaketh frowardness."—Proverbs 10:31,32.

"And the speech pleased the Lord, that Solomon had
asked this thing."—I Kings 3:10.

"A soft answer turneth away wrath: but grievous words
stir up anger. The tongue of the wise useth knowledge aright:
but the mouth of fools poureth out foolishness....A whole-
some tongue is a tree of life: but perverseness therein is a
breach in the spirit."—Proverbs 15:1,2,4.

"If any man among you seem to be religious, and bridleth
not his tongue, but deceiveth his own heart, this man's religion is vain."—James 1:26.

139

GET A GRIP!

"Whoso keepeth his mouth and his tongue keepeth his soul from troubles."—Proverbs 21:23.

"Excellent speech becometh not a fool: much less do lying lips a prince."—Proverbs 17:7.

"He that covereth a transgression seeketh love; but he that repeateth a matter separateth very friends."—Proverbs 17:9.

"He that hath knowledge spareth his words: and a man of understanding is of an excellent spirit."—Proverbs 17:27.

"Let no corrupt communication proceed out of your mouth, but that which is good to the use of edifying, that it may minister grace unto the hearers."—Ephesians 4:29.

"Let your speech be alway with grace, seasoned with salt, that ye may know how ye ought to answer every man."—Colossians 4:6.

"Sound speech, that cannot be condemned; that he that is of the contrary part may be ashamed, having no evil thing to say of you."—Titus 2:8.

"In the mouth of the foolish is a rod of pride: but the lips of the wise shall preserve them."—Proverbs 14:3.

The tongue is the greatest of blessings when wisely and lovingly used, but it becomes the greatest curse when it is unkindly and dishonestly used.

–A. Purnell Bailey

SPIRITUAL GROWTH

Progressing in one's efforts to live according to
God's guidelines as set down in His Word.

*"How much better is it to get wisdom than gold! and to
get understanding rather to be chosen than silver!"* —
Proverbs 16:16.

*"We are bound to thank God always for you, brethren,
as it is meet, because that your faith groweth exceedingly,
and the charity of every one of you all toward each other
aboundeth."* —II Thessalonians 1:3.

*"Finally, my brethren, be strong in the Lord, and in the
power of his might. Put on the whole armour of God, that ye
may be able to stand against the wiles of the devil. For we
wrestle not against flesh and blood, but against principalities, against powers, against the rulers of the darkness of
this world, against spiritual wickedness in high places.
Wherefore take unto you the whole armour of God, that
ye may be able to withstand in the evil day, and having
done all, to stand. Stand therefore, having your loins girt
about with truth, and having on the breastplate of righteousness."* —Ephesians 6:10–14.

*"But grow in grace, and in the knowledge of our Lord and
Saviour Jesus Christ. To him be glory both now and for ever.
Amen."* —II Peter 3:18.

*"Study to shew thyself approved unto God, a workman
that needeth not to be ashamed, rightly dividing the word of
truth."* —II Timothy 2:15.

*"A man's heart deviseth his way: but the LORD directeth
his steps."* —Proverbs 16:9.

"But continue thou in the things which thou hast learned and hast been assured of, knowing of whom thou hast learned them; And that from a child thou hast known the holy scriptures, which are able to make thee wise unto salvation through faith which is in Christ Jesus."— II Timothy 3:14, 15.

"The heart of the wise teacheth his mouth, and addeth learning to his lips."—Proverbs 16:23.

"That Christ may dwell in your hearts by faith; that ye, being rooted and grounded in love, May be able to comprehend with all saints what is the breadth, and length, and depth, and height; And to know the love of Christ, which passeth knowledge, that ye might be filled with all the fulness of God."—Ephesians 3:17–19.

"As newborn babes, desire the sincere milk of the word, that ye may grow thereby: If so be ye have tasted that the Lord is gracious."—I Peter 2:2, 3.

"Apply thine heart unto instruction, and thine ears to the words of knowledge."—Proverbs 23:12.

We don't have to fight or wrestle with God, but we must wrestle before God with things. Beware of lazily giving up. Instead, put up a glorious fight, and you will find yourself empowered with His strength.

—Oswald Chambers

SUCCESS

Success is not always visible, and achieving it is more mental then physical.

"This book of the law shall not depart out of thy mouth; but thou shalt meditate therein day and night, that thou mayest observe to do according to all that is written therein: for then thou shalt make thy way prosperous, and then thou shalt have good success." —Joshua 1:8.

"And let us not be weary in well doing: for in due season we shall reap, if we faint not." —Galatians 6:9.

"Therefore, my beloved brethren, be ye stedfast, unmoveable, always abounding in the work of the Lord, forasmuch as ye know that your labour is not in vain in the Lord." — I Corinthians 15:58.

"Know ye not that they which run in a race run all, but one receiveth the prize? So run, that ye may obtain. And every man that striveth for the mastery is temperate in all things. Now they do it to obtain a corruptible crown; but we an incorruptible." —I Corinthians 9:24,25.

"Commit thy works unto the LORD, and thy thoughts shall be established." —Proverbs 16:3.

"Knowing that whatsoever good thing any man doeth, the same shall he receive of the Lord, whether he be bond or free." —Ephesians 6:8.

"By humility and the fear of the LORD are riches, and honour, and life." —Proverbs 22:4.

143

"But it shall not be so among you: but whosoever will be great among you, let him be your minister."—Matthew 20:26.

"The hand of the diligent shall bear rule: but the slothful shall be under tribute."—Proverbs 12:24.

"Study to shew thyself approved unto God, a workman that needeth not to be ashamed, rightly dividing the word of truth."—II Timothy 2:15.

"Every man also to whom God hath given riches and wealth, and hath given him power to eat thereof, and to take his portion, and to rejoice in his labour; this is the gift of God."—Ecclesiastes 5:19.

There are no secrets to success. It is the result of preparation, hard work and learning from failure.

–Colin Powell

Success is never final, and failure, never fatal. It's courage that counts.

–George Tilton

TEMPTATION

A real test of your spiritual character. During these times, you need the truth of God's Word more than ever.

"And lead us not into temptation, but deliver us from evil: For thine is the kingdom, and the power, and the glory, for ever. Amen."—Matthew 6:13.

"Put on the whole armour of God, that ye may be able to stand against the wiles of the devil."—Ephesians 6:11.

"But evil men and seducers shall wax worse and worse, deceiving, and being deceived."—II Timothy 3:13.

"Submit yourselves therefore to God. Resist the devil, and he will flee from you."—James 4:7.

"My son, if sinners entice thee, consent thou not."—Proverbs 1:10.

"Let not sin therefore reign in your mortal body, that ye should obey it in the lusts thereof. Neither yield ye your members as instruments of unrighteousness unto sin: but yield yourselves unto God, as those that are alive from the dead, and your members as instruments of righteousness unto God."—Romans 6:12,13.

"Enter not into the path of the wicked, and go not in the way of evil men. Avoid it, pass not by it, turn from it, and pass away."—Proverbs 4:14,15.

"Let no man say when he is tempted, I am tempted of God: for God cannot be tempted with evil, neither tempteth he any man. But every man is tempted, when he is drawn away of his own lust, and enticed."—James 1:13,14.

145

"Whoso causeth the righteous to go astray in an evil way, he shall fall himself into his own pit: but the upright shall have good things in possession."—Proverbs 28:10.

"For the grace of God that bringeth salvation hath appeared to all men, Teaching us that, denying ungodliness and worldly lusts, we should live soberly, righteously, and godly, in this present world."—Titus 2:11,12.

"My brethren, count it all joy when ye fall into divers temptations; Knowing this, that the trying of your faith worketh patience."—James 1:2,3.

"There hath no temptation taken you but such as is common to man: but God is faithful, who will not suffer you to be tempted above that ye are able; but will with the temptation also make a way to escape, that ye may be able to bear it."—I Corinthians 10:13.

Temptations, unlike opportunities, will always give you many second chances.

—O. A. Battista

THOUGHTS

Where you really live—really!
Some are intentional, while others are not.

"Casting down imaginations, and every high thing that exalteth itself against the knowledge of God, and bringing into captivity every thought to the obedience of Christ."—II Corinthians 10:5.

"The thought of foolishness is sin: and the scorner is an abomination to men."—Proverbs 24:9.

"For who hath known the mind of the Lord, that he may instruct him? But we have the mind of Christ."—I Corinthians 2:16.

"But so much the more went there a fame abroad of him: and great multitudes came together to hear, and to be healed by him of their infirmities. And he withdrew himself into the wilderness, and prayed."—Luke 5:15,16.

"A merry heart doeth good like a medicine: but a broken spirit drieth the bones."—Proverbs 17:22.

"And be not conformed to this world: but be ye transformed by the renewing of your mind, that ye may prove what is that good, and acceptable, and perfect, will of God."—Romans 12:2.

"For the word of God is quick, and powerful, and sharper than any twoedged sword, piercing even to the dividing asunder of soul and spirit, and of the joints and marrow, and is a discerner of the thoughts and intents of the heart."—Hebrews 4:12.

147

GET A GRIP!

"Let the wicked forsake his way, and the unrighteous man his thoughts: and let him return unto the LORD, and he will have mercy upon him; and to our God, for he will abundantly pardon. For my thoughts are not your thoughts, neither are your ways my ways, saith the LORD. For as the heavens are higher than the earth, so are my ways higher than your ways, and my thoughts than your thoughts."—Isaiah 55:7–9.

"If ye then be risen with Christ, seek those things which are above, where Christ sitteth on the right hand of God. Set your affection on things above, not on things on the earth."—Colossians 3:1,2.

"The thoughts of the righteous are right: but the counsels of the wicked are deceit."—Proverbs 12:5.

"And again, The Lord knoweth the thoughts of the wise, that they are vain."—I Corinthians 3:20.

"I know that thou canst do every thing, and that no thought can be withholden from thee."—Job 42:2.

"The LORD knoweth the thoughts of man, that they are vanity."—Psalm 94:11.

Every deed, whether good or evil, was conceived in the thought process of the mind.
–Lindsay Terry

TIME

What your life consists of.

"Walk in wisdom toward them that are without, redeeming the time."—Colossians 4:5.

"And as he reasoned of righteousness, temperance, and judgment to come, Felix trembled, and answered, Go thy way for this time; when I have a convenient season, I will call for thee."—Acts 24:25.

"He that tilleth his land shall be satisfied with bread: but he that followeth vain persons is void of understanding."—Proverbs 12:11.

"So teach us to number our days, that we may apply our hearts unto wisdom."—Psalm 90:12.

"And that, knowing the time, that now it is high time to awake out of sleep: for now is our salvation nearer than when we believed."—Romans 13:11.

"Six days shalt thou labour, and do all thy work: But the seventh day is the sabbath of the LORD thy God: in it thou shalt not do any work, thou, nor thy son, nor thy daughter, thy manservant, nor thy maidservant, nor thy cattle, nor thy stranger that is within thy gates."—Exodus 20:9, 10.

"Rejoice, O young man, in thy youth; and let thy heart cheer thee in the days of thy youth, and walk in the ways of thine heart, and in the sight of thine eyes: but know thou, that for all these things God will bring thee into judgment."—Ecclesiastes 11:9.

"Redeeming the time, because the days are evil."—Ephesians 5:16.

"For he saith, I have heard thee in a time accepted, and in the day of salvation have I succoured thee: behold, now is the accepted time; behold, now is the day of salvation."—II Corinthians 6:2.

"Sow to yourselves in righteousness, reap in mercy; break up your fallow ground: for it is time to seek the LORD, till he come and rain righteousness upon you."—Hosea 10:12.

"Repent ye therefore, and be converted, that your sins may be blotted out, when the times of refreshing shall come from the presence of the Lord."—Acts 3:19.

"Thus saith the LORD, In an acceptable time have I heard thee, and in a day of salvation have I helped thee: and I will preserve thee, and give thee for a covenant of the people, to establish the earth, to cause to inherit the desolate heritages."—Isaiah 49:8.

Our greatest danger in life is in permitting the urgent things to crowd out the important.

–Charles E. Hummel

TRUTHFULNESS

That which knows no part of a lie.

"I have chosen the way of truth: thy judgments have I laid before me."—Psalm 119:30.

"He is the Rock, his work is perfect: for all his ways are judgment: a God of truth and without iniquity, just and right is he."—Deuteronomy 32:4.

"The lip of truth shall be established for ever: but a lying tongue is but for a moment."—Proverbs 12:19.

"A man that beareth false witness against his neighbour is a maul, and a sword, and a sharp arrow."—Proverbs 25:18.

"He that walketh uprightly, and worketh righteousness, and speaketh the truth in his heart."—Psalm 15:2.

"He that speaketh truth sheweth forth righteousness: but a false witness deceit."—Proverbs 12:17.

"These are the things that ye shall do; Speak ye every man the truth to his neighbour; execute the judgment of truth and peace in your gates."—Zechariah 8:16.

"A true witness delivereth souls: but a deceitful witness speaketh lies."—Proverbs 14:25.

"Jesus saith unto him, I am the way, the truth, and the life: no man cometh unto the Father, but by me."—John 14:6.

"But speaking the truth in love, may grow up into him in all things, which is the head, even Christ."—Ephesians 4:15.

GET A GRIP!

"Howbeit when he, the Spirit of truth, is come, he will guide you into all truth: for he shall not speak of himself; but whatsoever he shall hear, that shall he speak: and he will shew you things to come."—John 16:13.

"And ye shall know the truth, and the truth shall make you free."—John 8:32.

"Study to shew thyself approved unto God, a workman that needeth not to be ashamed, rightly dividing the word of truth."—II Timothy 2:15.

"Rejoiceth not in iniquity, but rejoiceth in the truth."—I Corinthians 13:6.

"For of this sort are they which creep into houses, and lead captive silly women laden with sins, led away with divers lusts, Ever learning, and never able to come to the knowledge of the truth."—II Timothy 3:6, 7.

The truth is incontrovertible. Malice may attack it. Ignorance may deride it. But in the end, there it is.
—Winston Churchill

When you stretch the truth, watch out for the snapback.
—Bill Copeland

152

WILL OF GOD

God has a plan for your life and mine.

"*Trust in the* LORD *with all thine heart; and lean not unto thine own understanding. In all thy ways acknowledge him, and he shall direct thy paths.*"—Proverbs 3:5,6.

"*Of his own will begat he us with the word of truth, that we should be a kind of firstfruits of his creatures.*"—James 1:18.

"*And when he would not be persuaded, we ceased, saying, The will of the Lord be done.*"—Acts 21:14.

"*But the fruit of the Spirit is love, joy, peace, longsuffering, gentleness, goodness, faith. Meekness, temperance: against such there is no law.*"—Galatians 5:22,23.

"*Thou compassest my path and my lying down, and art acquainted with all my ways.*"—Psalm 139:3.

"*Yea, if thou criest after knowledge, and liftest up thy voice for understanding; If thou seekest her as silver, and searchest for her as for hid treasures; Then shalt thou understand the fear of the* LORD, *and find the knowledge of God. For the* LORD *giveth wisdom: out of his mouth cometh knowledge and understanding.*"—Proverbs 2:3–6.

"*I will instruct thee and teach thee in the way which thou shalt go: I will guide thee with mine eye.*"—Psalm 32:8.

"*And this is the confidence that we have in him, that, if we ask any thing according to his will, he heareth us.*"—I John 5:14.

"For it is God which worketh in you both to will and to do of his good pleasure."—Philippians 2:13.

"For whosoever shall do the will of God, the same is my brother, and my sister, and mother."—Mark 3:35.

"The LORD will perfect that which concerneth me: thy mercy, O LORD, endureth for ever: forsake not the works of thine own hands."—Psalm 138:8.

"In whom also we have obtained an inheritance, being predestinated according to the purpose of him who worketh all things after the counsel of his own will."—Ephesians 1:11.

"God also bearing them witness, both with signs and wonders, and with divers miracles, and gifts of the Holy Ghost, according to his own will?"—Hebrews 2:4.

Never be afraid to do what God tells you to do—it's always good.

—Malcolm Cronk

WITNESSING

Telling others, as groups or as individuals, the good
news of Jesus and His love for the souls of men.

*"And Jesus said unto them, Come ye after me, and I will
make you to become fishers of men."*—Mark 1:17.

*"And daily in the temple, and in every house, they ceased
not to teach and preach Jesus Christ."*—Acts 5:42.

*"And that repentance and remission of sins should be
preached in his name among all nations, beginning at
Jerusalem."*—Luke 24:47.

*"And he commanded us to preach unto the people, and to
testify that it is he which was ordained of God to be the
Judge of quick and dead."*—Acts 10:42.

*"Let the redeemed of the LORD say so, whom he hath
redeemed from the hand of the enemy."*—Psalm 107:2.

*"And he said unto them, Go ye into all the world, and
preach the gospel to every creature."*—Mark 16:15.

*"And others save with fear, pulling them out of the fire;
hating even the garment spotted by the flesh."*—Jude 23.

*"And they that be wise shall shine as the brightness of the
firmament; and they that turn many to righteousness as the
stars for ever and ever."*—Daniel 12:3.

*"And with great power gave the apostles witness of the
resurrection of the Lord Jesus: and great grace was upon
them all."*—Acts 4:33.

"How then shall they call on him in whom they have not believed? and how shall they believe in him of whom they have not heard? and how shall they hear without a preacher? And how shall they preach, except they be sent? as it is written, How beautiful are the feet of them that preach the gospel of peace, and bring glad tidings of good things!" — Romans 10:14,15.

"But sanctify the Lord God in your hearts: and be ready always to give an answer to every man that asketh you a reason of the hope that is in you with meekness and fear." — I Peter 3:15.

"For our gospel came not unto you in word only, but also in power, and in the Holy Ghost, and in much assurance; as ye know what manner of men we were among you for your sake." — I Thessalonians 1:5.

"And the lord said unto the servant, Go out into the highways and hedges, and compel them to come in, that my house may be filled." — Luke 14:23.

"Preach the word; be instant in season, out of season; reprove, rebuke, exhort with all longsuffering and doctrine." — II Timothy 4:2.

The world is far more ready to receive the Gospel than Christians are to hand it out.

—George W. Peters

WORK

The Heavenly Father watches every task with much greater
interest than we may realize. We work to obtain necessary
food, clothing and shelter; and we work for our Lord.
Consider also the work of the Father.

"Let him that stole steal no more: but rather let him
labour, working with his hands the thing which is good, that
he may have to give to him that needeth."—Ephesians 4:28.

"For even when we were with you, this we commanded
you, that if any would not work, neither should he eat."—
II Thessalonians 3:10.

"And the men did the work faithfully."—II Chronicles
34:12.

"Hast not thou made an hedge about him, and about his
house, and about all that he hath on every side? thou hast
blessed the work of his hands, and his substance is
increased in the land."—Job 1:10.

"I remember the days of old; I meditate on all thy works;
I muse on the work of thy hands."—Psalm 143:5.

"When I consider thy heavens, the work of thy fingers, the
moon and the stars, which thou hast ordained."—Psalm 8:3.

"It is time for thee, LORD, to work: for they have made void
thy law."—Psalm 119:126.

"Go to the ant, thou sluggard; consider her ways, and be
wise."—Proverbs 6:6.

GET A GRIP!

"The soul of the sluggard desireth, and hath nothing: but the soul of the diligent shall be made fat."—Proverbs 13:4.

"Man goeth forth unto his work and to his labour until the evening."—Psalm 104:23.

"Commit thy works unto the LORD, and thy thoughts shall be established."—Proverbs 16:3.

"And that ye study to be quiet, and to do your own business, and to work with your own hands, as we commanded you."—I Thessalonians 4:11.

"As vinegar to the teeth, and as smoke to the eyes, so is the sluggard to them that send him."—Proverbs 10:26.

"The sluggard will not plow by reason of the cold; therefore shall he beg in harvest, and have nothing."—Proverbs 20:4.

The number of people who are unemployed isn't as great as the number who aren't working.

—Frank A. Clark

WORRY

Troubling thoughts and anxiety.

"Be careful for nothing; but in every thing by prayer and supplication with thanksgiving let your requests be made known unto God. And the peace of God, which passeth all understanding, shall keep your hearts and minds through Christ Jesus."—Philippians 4:6,7.

"For God hath not given us the spirit of fear; but of power, and of love, and of a sound mind."—II Timothy 1:7.

"Humble yourselves therefore under the mighty hand of God, that he may exalt you in due time: Casting all your care upon him; for he careth for you."—I Peter 5:6,7.

"Fret not thyself because of evildoers, neither be thou envious against the workers of iniquity."—Psalm 37:1.

"And Moses said unto the people, Fear ye not, stand still, and see the salvation of the LORD, *which he will shew to you to day: for the Egyptians whom ye have seen to day, ye shall see them again no more for ever."*—Exodus 14:13.

"He only is my rock and my salvation: he is my defence; I shall not be moved."—Psalm 62:6.

"Therefore I say unto you, Take no thought for your life, what ye shall eat, or what ye shall drink; nor yet for your body, what ye shall put on. Is not the life more than meat, and the body than raiment?"—Matthew 6:25.

"Trust in the LORD, *and do good; so shalt thou dwell in the land, and verily thou shalt be fed."*—Psalm 37:3.

GET A GRIP!

"For the thing which I greatly feared is come upon me, and that which I was afraid of is come unto me."—Job 3:25.

"Rest in the LORD, and wait patiently for him: fret not thyself because of him who prospereth in his way, because of the man who bringeth wicked devices to pass."—Psalm 37:7.

"I will not be afraid of ten thousands of people, that have set themselves against me round about."—Psalm 3:6.

"The LORD is on my side; I will not fear: what can man do unto me?"—Psalm 118:6.

"When thou liest down, thou shalt not be afraid: yea, thou shalt lie down, and thy sleep shall be sweet."—Proverbs 3:24.

"Behold, God is my salvation; I will trust, and not be afraid: for the LORD JEHOVAH is my strength and my song; he also is become my salvation."—Isaiah 12:2.

"Take therefore no thought for the morrow: for the morrow shall take thought for the things of itself. Sufficient unto the day is the evil thereof."—Matthew 6:34.

**It is not the work, but the worry
that breaks the heart of a man.**
—Charles F. Weigle

WORSHIP

Worship is giving God the best He has given you.
—Oswald Chambers

"For we are the circumcision, which worship God in the spirit, and rejoice in Christ Jesus, and have no confidence in the flesh."—Philippians 3:3.

"And the man bowed down his head, and worshipped the LORD."—Genesis 24:26.

"I will worship toward thy holy temple, and praise thy name for thy lovingkindness and for thy truth: for thou hast magnified thy word above all thy name."—Psalm 138:2.

"And the people believed: and when they heard that the LORD had visited the children of Israel, and that he had looked upon their affliction, then they bowed their heads and worshipped."—Exodus 4:31.

"And he hath put a new song in my mouth, even praise unto our God: many shall see it, and fear, and shall trust in the LORD."—Psalm 40:3.

"Heal me, O LORD, and I shall be healed; save me, and I shall be saved: for thou art my praise."—Jeremiah 17:14.

"It came even to pass, as the trumpeters and singers were as one, to make one sound to be heard in praising and thanking the LORD; and when they lifted up their voice with the trumpets and cymbals and instruments of musick, and praised the LORD, saying, For he is good; for his mercy endureth for ever: that then the house was filled with a cloud, even the house of the LORD."—II Chronicles 5:13.

"And, behold, there came a leper and worshipped him, saying, Lord, if thou wilt, thou canst make me clean."— Matthew 8:2.

"By him therefore let us offer the sacrifice of praise to God continually, that is, the fruit of our lips giving thanks to his name."—Hebrews 13:15.

"I beseech you therefore, brethren, by the mercies of God, that ye present your bodies a living sacrifice, holy, acceptable unto God, which is your reasonable service."—Romans 12:1.

"Now we know that God heareth not sinners: but if any man be a worshipper of God, and doeth his will, him he heareth."—John 9:31.

"Thou, even thou, art LORD alone; thou hast made heaven, the heaven of heavens, with all their host, the earth, and all things that are therein, the seas, and all that is therein, and thou preservest them all; and the host of heaven worshippeth thee."—Nehemiah 9:6.

"But God forbid that I should glory, save in the cross of our Lord Jesus Christ, by whom the world is crucified unto me, and I unto the world."—Galatians 6:14.

"Praise ye the LORD. Praise God in his sanctuary: praise him in the firmament of his power."—Psalm 150:1.

A private relationship of worshiping God is the great essential element of spiritual fitness.
–Oswald Chambers

YOUTH

The young, vital, impressionable years.

"*Let no man despise thy youth; but be thou an example of the believers, in word, in conversation, in charity, in spirit, in faith, in purity.*"—I Timothy 4:12.

"*Flee also youthful lusts: but follow righteousness, faith, charity, peace, with them that call on the Lord out of a pure heart.*"—II Timothy 2:22.

"*Remember now thy Creator in the days of thy youth, while the evil days come not, nor the years draw nigh, when thou shalt say, I have no pleasure in them.*"—Ecclesiastes 12:1.

"*And in all thine abominations and thy whoredoms thou hast not remembered the days of thy youth, when thou wast naked and bare, and wast polluted in thy blood.*"—Ezekiel 16:22.

"*Remember not the sins of my youth, nor my transgressions: according to thy mercy remember thou me for thy goodness' sake, O LORD.*"—Psalm 25:7.

"*For thou art my hope, O Lord GOD: thou art my trust from my youth.*"—Psalm 71:5.

"*My manner of life from my youth, which was at the first among mine own nation at Jerusalem, know all the Jews.*"—Acts 26:4.

"*O God, thou hast taught me from my youth: and hitherto have I declared thy wondrous works.*"—Psalm 71:17.

GET A GRIP!

"Foolishness is bound in the heart of a child; but the rod of correction shall drive it far from him."—Proverbs 22:15.

"Whoso keepeth the law is a wise son: but he that is a companion of riotous men shameth his father."—Proverbs 28:7.

"That they may teach the young women to be sober, to love their husbands, to love their children."—Titus 2:4.

"Who satisfieth thy mouth with good things; so that thy youth is renewed like the eagle's."—Psalm 103:5.

One of the virtues of being very young is that you don't let the facts get in the way of your imagination.

—Sam Levenson